Living Your
Intuitive Dreams

Living Your Intuitive Dreams

A self-discovery workbook

sHEALy

Writers Club Press

San Jose New York Lincoln Shanghai

Living Your Intuitive Dreams
A self-discovery workbook

Writers Club Press
an imprint of iUniverse, Inc.

For information address:
iUniverse, Inc.
5220 S. 16th St., Suite 200
Lincoln, NE 68512
www.iuniverse.com

ISBN: 0-595-20807-X

Printed in the United States of America

This book is dedicated to my clients, the questioners of the world; those I have met in the past, and those I will meet in the future.

ACKNOWLEDGMENTS

I would like to acknowledge those who have been so helpful and loving to me while writing this book. Two angels, Crystal and Chase, were at my side each day waiting for me to complete this manuscript. They faithfully encouraged me and only smiled as I repeated to them daily, "This is a really good manuscript. I can't wait for you to read it".

Next, I would like to give special thanks to Chris who first edited this book for me. She was there when I most needed her; to Liz who also volunteered to share her journalistic skills with me and edit the final draft. Thank you Liz for being available to me.

It has become obvious to me that my friends are true friends, and that they are eager to help me when I am in need.

Also, I would like to thank Donna, who shared her magical life and poetry in chapter two. Although, the names of the individuals mentioned in this book, have been changed, the poetry recorded in chapter two is the work of Donna Clementoni. Congratulations, Donna, you have created the life of your intuitive dreams. (POET4POP@AOL.COM)

Lastly, I would like to acknowledge my husband, Pat, and my mother, Peggy. Thank you for being a never-ending support.

PREFACE

While writing I am embraced by the spirits of creativity, truth, love, hope, health, prosperity and serenity. They are like sisters to me. Surprisingly, my deceased great grandmother, Stella, found her voice and now speaks to me through these pages. She continues to encourage me to use my psychic abilities and she encourage others like me to use theirs. I also am visited by a magical and charming realm of young angelic energies who have begun to guide me and to answer the new questions I ponder. They have found a way to speak to you through me.

As you peruse the following pages and exercises you, too, will be embraced by loving energies and the world of spirit. The distribution of this workbook has given new life and energy to them.

Working with the psychic world I have had opportunities to see some of the mysteries of life and I have learned to live intuitively. Intuition is laced to each aspect of my life. Intuition is my common sense and my good judgment and the force that helps me make my dreams come true. There was a time when I struggled with my own belief system. I had learned through the church and church leaders that my psychic abilities were unnatural and considered unorthodox. I attempted to hide them from others for much of my young life. In private, I found my intuitions to be the most helpful resources I possessed, but in public I pretended that they did not exist. I felt shamed by those who did not understand me, but eventually I met people who, like me, had the gift of intuition, and I began to educate myself under their guidance. I came to realize that intuition is a normal part of human existence and that all of us have it to some extent. As I became more comfortable with my own psychic abilities they grew and led me to understand their value. I realized that intuition comes only from Godly energies and that those who fear it are only ignorant to a source of healing. I began living without fear of using my psychic abilities and eventually found a voice and words that others wanted to hear. Now, I am grateful for the struggles I endured because I am better able to empathize with others on a similar path. I also am able to share the insights of Universal love and basic information I have learned.

Although I have struggled and become lost at times, today I know that one of my life's destinations is to help prevent you from doing the same. I have discovered the depth and possibilities of living the life of my intuitive dreams. And today my life is a life of which many others only dream. I hope to share this wealth of knowledge with you. You can make changes in your life, as I did. Your dreams can come true!

INTRODUCTION

You are more than the physical body and skin in which you were born. You are a living spirit who will live on in eternity, forever. But here, today, you strive to create the life that you want to live. So many people sit back and let life pass them by; they only dream of a good life. They hope to have happiness and more but somehow it seems to slip through their fingers. You don't have to be one who lets life slip away from you. Take hold of your dreams and make them come true. It's possible when you learn to use your intuition properly. First, recognize your thoughts and desires as intuitive messages directing you toward your highest destination. Then, learn to live each day in touch with your intuition.

This book will introduce you to your own natural intuitive abilities and exercises that will enhance them. If you focus your efforts on the one simple goal of developing your intuitive abilities, you will discover that once you learn to use them properly they automatically guide you toward the life you want and dream. As a matter of fact, today you can begin to identify the aspects of your life that you would like to change. Perhaps you think that these changes are impossible to achieve, well, not true. You can achieve anything you want and all you need to do while working through this manuscript is focus on one goal—developing your natural intuitive abilities.

As you begin to recognize your intuitive potentials, opportunities to achieve all that you desire and deserve will present themselves. Love, health and prosperity are fruits of life; and they are yours for the taking when you focus your intuition. Have you ever wondered why some people seem to achieve so much while others only struggle? Think of all the high achievers you know. They have one thing in common. They know what they want and how to go after it. As you read through each chapter and practice the exercises made available to you in this manuscript you will learn about five godly energies, clairvoyance, earth spirituality, soul mate encounters, the pursuit of prosperity and your own ability to connect with these aspects of life.

Your spirit, striving to grow and love is beautiful and affluent just because it exists, and it is connected to an intuitive world of knowledge, angel energies, spirits and earthly cycles. Here, you will learn more about these wonderful gifts and your ability to intuitively connect to them. Read through this manuscript, take in the information without judging it, and work through the exercises that are available to you. Three journals have been provided for you to record your dreams, thoughts and intuitive impressions. Use these journals every day until you have completed all of the exercises given to you and filled all of the journal pages. Then put this book away in a private place. Do not look at it for a few weeks but continue to live practicing your new abilities. Then, go back to this book and read it again. You will have a new understanding of much of the basic information that is provided. Read over your own journal writings at this time and you will be amazed at the psychic information that you have clearly recorded.

In time, you will begin to recognize positive changes in the direction your life is moving. You will realize that you have become the intuitive director of your own life and that you have recognized amazing connections to a miraculous and spiritual world which allows you to create the life you have previously only dreamed.

Your imagination is the next step toward developing your intuition. Imagine a phenomenal career, the true love of your life, refined psychic abilities, genuine friendships and a commitment to living your life to its fullest. Do you like what you see?

Once you can imagine yourself in a better life, you will learn to use an aspect of intuition called clairvoyance to decide the correct path you are to take to achieve these goals. You will learn to make good choices and create affluent situations by trusting these insights. Also, it is possible to develop extrasensory perceptions that will help you develop the ability to see the beautiful colors of the human aura as well as the aura of the spirit world. This book, however, will focus mainly upon its original goal: helping you to develop the intuitive abilities that will lead you toward improving your practical life. But, don't be surprised if you begin to experience unusual circumstances and sights as you work to improve your life. You will learn to channel information that will guide you toward improving your life's path and to use this skill as an intuitive method to better know your inner self. You will become familiar with the term "gnostic", to know, and you will learn that it is possible to know what choices and circumstances are best for yourself. While getting to know yourself and your surroundings intuitively, you also will learn to easily connect with psychic energies. You already do this daily, but it is possible for you to enhance this connection. You will discover the power of your own thoughts, conscious and unconscious, and, you will learn to direct your unconscious as well as your conscious thoughts.

You will no longer know only your physical body. You will intuitively begin to embrace your spirit. No longer will you only dream of a good life. Today, you are beginning to create one.

CONTENTS

Do something magical today!

Part One

Chapter One

Psychic Living

A spirit called Serenity is sitting comfortably in the corner of my office about three feet away from me. Apparently, she is happy with the work I am doing today. The thoughts and words I often struggle to record are flowing freely from my pen upon paper now. I know she is helping me, guiding my thoughts, sharing with me important messages.

While writing this manuscript she, and others like her, remind me that you will be reading and learning from my words. She shows me that you are part of a busy and sometimes cold world and that you might need a little encouragement toward change. She reminds me that you often dream of a better life for yourself and that you desire to be more than what you are today. You desire and deserve a rich spirituality, a connection with nature, loving relationships, good health and prosperity.

All of these can be yours when you learn one simple lesson; you must learn to live using your intuition because your intuition will help you create the life of which you dream. Simply, you must begin living your intuitive dreams. This chapter will introduce you to your own psychic strengths. Read through this chapter and follow the exercises provided.

I encourage you to work through this manuscript as if you are uncovering new pieces of yourself and expect to give birth to the life of which you only have dreamed. Developing your psychic abilities and learning to live using these abilities will help you gain new perspectives on all things you encounter. You will be a new and refreshed soul with the ability to create a new and powerful life filled with adventure.

To develop your intuition you will first study five psychic energy sources that are a part of the universe. They are referred to as, The Realm of Thought, The Realm of Spirit, The Realm of Angels, The Realm of God and the Realm of Magic.

As you work through the exercises provided in this chapter you will have small glimpses of these realms and simultaneously your intuition will begin to develop. Each of these realms, a part of nature, offers a unique energy. You have undoubtedly connected with a few of them. Take your time as you begin this work. Intuition will grow throughout your lifetime but you will begin to see your own amazing skills immediately.

Connecting to the Realms

Your psychic energies are connected to the five realms. Each realm is a force of nature with its own unique attribute and power. Like a tapestry, they entwine together, creating everything that you call life. They are the life forces you see in action when the spring trees bloom or when a baby is born. You feel them when you fall in love or when you long to embrace the greater meaning of life. They are around you, filling your lungs with life right now. They are extraordinary and real and it makes sense to learn more about them and to attempt to keep a secure connection with them. Why would you not make use of these energies when attempting to direct your life along a better path? If you are seeking to improve yourself you will want to use every opportunity available. And these energies are available to you whenever you ask for their assistance. Traditionally, humans have connected to this energy through the services of spiritual leaders and organized institutions; churches, synagogues, and temples. These institutions are all that some people need but you may long to take this opportunity to go beyond the orthodox and explore nature and spirit on a more intrinsic level.

There are multitudes of ways in which to begin your quest to connect to these energies. Attempting a few simple exercises using meditation, channeling and journal writing will start you on the path of developing your intuition and as your psychic abilities are enhanced you will begin to clearly experience the five realms of energy.

Realm Of Thought

The first and easiest energy source in which to connect is the realm of thought. The realm of thought is often the first connection into psychic experiences because it holds the collective unconscious of all the beings of the world. It is the realm that holds all of the information that human beings have thought and learned throughout the ages. Imagine a mass of intelligence or genius collectively bound together forming actual thought forms and synchronicities. Imagine connecting to this realm and being linked to ideas and motivations that once influenced world leaders or sages. It is possible to effectively do this when using your psychic abilities. Make an attempt to connect to this realm and it acts like a running stream washing ideas and thoughts over you. This energy helps keep human beings connected as a species. You can tap into it each day as you make decisions or converse with other people. When you make a conscious decision to connect to this energy you will increase your abilities to understand the motivation and desires of other people as well as your own thought and decision processes. Once you have begun to increase your connection to this realm you will notice that you can converse with others more easily, make friendships more easily and present yourself in a more positive manner. People will be more attracted to you because you have the ability to listen and to perceive.

This realm is often responsible for individuals who have found it possible to read minds. Intuitive individuals often first connect here before continuing on to experience other modes of psychic communication and deepen their gift of insight. I recall a story an old friend shared with me. One hot summer day, Charlotte and her four sons visited an amusement park. Each of her sons decided to go his own way leaving my friend, Charlotte to walk around the park and do a little sight seeing and shopping. A few hours later my friend began to feel a little faint and eventually decided that she needed to sit down to rest. After resting a few minutes she began feeling even more tired and out of breathe. The day was extremely hot and breathing conditions were unusually harsh. She was tired and wanted to go home but her sons were no place to be seen and there was another hour before they would meet at the front gate to go home, as they had planned. The park, approximately five miles wide, was crowded with people and noisy amusement rides. So, my friend decided to try a trick that she had recently learned. She began to visualize the face of each son. With concentration, she was able to see the face of each boy and imagine his location as well. She continued to focus on the vision available to her until she felt that she could see each boy clearly. She did not question or judge her abilities as she imagined each son in his specific location; she just continued to focus until she felt that each son was clearly in her thoughts. Than, she attempted to send a message to each of them. She started to concentrate on the phrase; "Meet your mother, now at the front gate." She continued to visualize the boys and send the message to them as she walked to the main entrance of the park. It took her about 15 minutes to get to the front of the park, but on her way she met two of her sons. Both boys explained to her that they had gotten tired and suddenly felt the desire to look for her. Now, when they reached the main gate, to all of their delight another one of the brothers was at the gate waiting. He, too, explained that he had felt a sudden desire to go home. Apparently, all of the sons, except for one, the youngest, had been receptive to the telepathic signal sent from mother. Later, on the ride home the three boys asked the youngest son where he had been during the last hour of his visit to the amusement park. The youngest son replied, "I was in the front of a line waiting to get on a water ride when I started to feel as if I wanted to turn around and go home. I would have gotten out of line and tried to find everybody sooner, but there was no way to exit from the front of the line. I stayed in line another 15 minutes and than got on the ride. It took me almost a half an hour to reach the front gate after that point."

My friend was delighted that all of her boys had heard the message that she had sent them. She tells me that still today she continues to use her thoughts as a means to contact her sons.

You have undoubtedly connected to this realm in your daily experiences already and use the insight available as a foundation for making common-sense decision. Common sense and knowledge are sisters of this energy realm. You use them hand in hand; without realizing that you have tapped into a psychic energy source. If you have ever met someone and felt a first impression that is either very negative or very positive you are connecting with this energy. If you have ever felt that someone is being dishonest or hiding something from you, you are connecting with this energy.

You are aware of your own thoughts and sometimes you can just as easily recognize the thoughts of others; you are already intuiting the thoughts of those around you. In fact, most of us are able to discern what others are thinking most of the time with just a little effort, but we do not trust our own instincts and do not take the time to think through much of our perceived information. Society has not taught you to stop and think about what thoughts and energies are flowing around you. You just let them flow and you chose to ignore them, quickly forget about them, or let them turn into worry. Sadly, many people use worry as a means to store some of their intuitive information. This is an unhealthy way to use your intuition but with a little effort you can make changes that will release this stress. Some individuals with a tendency to worry are actually very psychic by nature. They feel and intuit ideas but can become over taxed by the flow of information. This information seeps into their unconscious and becomes worry. Developing the psychic channels can solve this problem by creating a necessary outlet.

Begin to trust your inner voice. If you feel that someone is telling you only half of a truth or giving you only part of a message take the time to stop and listen to your own instincts. Trust yourself and believe that your intuitions are correct and sending signals that might be helpful.

Stop and respond appropriately. Ask questions if necessary but don't chose to ignore your instincts.

The following exercises are basic lessons to help prepare you to recognize your own intuitive abilities and to help you connect with an energy source that is easily accessible. Work through the exercises below. Perform as many of them as possible. They will help you change your daily perceptions. You do not have to do all of the exercises immediately. Take your time. Begin doing some of the exercises now while saving others for the appropriate time. If you are committed to changing your life through the use of intuition, the time for all of the exercises will make itself available to you.

Psychic Exercises

1. Begin to record all of your dreams in the specified section of this manuscript.

2. Develop a ritual that you can perform each night before going to bed. It can be simple. You might light a candle each night and think about the dreams you have dreamed earlier in the week. Or, you could spend time reading your dream book before turning out your lights and going to sleep.

3. Use the specified section of this manuscript as a journal for writing your thoughts. Record both skeptical and optimistic thoughts you may have concerning your intuitive abilities.

4. Repeat this simple chant as you fall asleep.
   "Thought Chant"
   Thoughts and Air I cannot see.
   Thoughts and Air come her to me.
   Intimate voices, in your minds eye.
   Intimate voices, flow through the sky.

A kasha Records, free to see.
A kasha Records, come to me.
A kasha Records, free to see.
A kasha Records, come to me.

5. As you wake each morning take a few minutes to organize your thoughts. Prioritize them in order from most to least important. Writing your thoughts on paper will be most effective and will help you focus on your most important goals and relieve you from worrying about things that are unimportant. Once you have organized your thoughts you will be more carefree and better able to receive messages that are around you.

6. Create a ritual to help you increase your ability to intuit the thoughts of others; purchase a light colored piece of satin fabric. Gold, light green, tangerine or silver will work best to remind you of the goal you are attempting to achieve. Turn the satin fabric inside out and begin to sew using violet thread. Sew the fabric into a bag shape. When you have completed the bag turn it right side out. Now fill the bag with dried lavender. Sew the bag closed with violet thread. Place the bag near the doorway you use to enter and exit your home. As you exit or enter your home you will smell the lavender and be reminded to focus your attentions on the thoughts of others.

7. Remember that other people like to hear themselves speak. They like to talk about themselves and they like to have a good listener as a friend. Try to spend more time listening to people and less time speaking. You will soon discover that you learn a lot about human nature. You will begin to hear many messages that are life affirming.

8. Invite friends to your home and hold a thought ritual. As two or more friends gather together, healing energies develop. Sit in a circle and hold hands. Each person should take time to express inner thoughts. Sometimes you will find yourself laughing instead

of speaking, but sometimes you will find yourself holding back tears. You will soon find that your friendships are tightened and your intuitive abilities are strengthened just from sharing energies with others.

9. On a new moon, record your own voice on a tape recorder. Speak into the recorder and release all of your thoughts. Be aware that you never have to share this tape with another person, so be free and let it all out. Then, listen to the tape and you will notice that you feel refreshed. Now you are ready to intuit the thoughts of others.

10. The best way to increase your abilities to intuit others' thoughts is to use the ability as often as possible. As you converse with others be open and express to them that you think you know what is on their minds Share these thoughts and see what happens. You will be pleasantly surprised.

11. Meditate to the sound "ohm". Clear your mind from all other distractions.

12. Practice deep breathing. Wait and listen to the world of spirit and angels to speak to you. They will connect to you by sharing their knowledge when they feel you are ready to hear. If you have made the decision to work hard and learn as much as possible about intuition they will share with you when your mind is quiet. So, wait and listen in silence.

13. Spend a large part of a day in silence. Do not speak. Keep the radio, cell phone, television and any other noisy devices turned off. Attempt to spend a few hours each week in this mode of silence. As you continue this exercise you will be tempted to write information that you are thinking and perceiving. Write only if the information seems to be coming from an intuitive voice. Do not record the obsessions or noise that is emptying from your mind.

Realm of Spirit

The realm of Spirit allows us to connect with our ancestors through memories, dreams, feelings, visions, and sound. It is easiest to peek into this realm when meditating or dreaming or in a trance. Mediums or psychics who have learned to connect to this realm are able to see into the future and divine the unknown. It is necessary, however to remember that this realm is filled with spirits who don't always know all of the answers. Some spirits are cloudy and vague with very little energy to share. Be careful when making a connection. Always look for someone here who is loving, kind, and trying to be helpful. With practice you will learn to decipher which spirit energies are helpful and which are not. Often you will connect with your own deceased family members and ancestors, or you may be able to develop a relationship with a spirit who desires to work as a spirit guide.

You have an unconscious connection to this realm right now and there are wonderful spirits waiting there to guide you. When you increase your connection you will see an immense psychic leap and you will have new skills to help with your practical daily life too.

As you make your way through your daily routine you will feel pushed to go in certain directions. This sensation will be the presence and influence of spirit energies. You will also sense that energy is available to persuade you to stay away from certain people and certain situations. Once again, this feeling is the presence of the spirit world. You will learn to trust this feeling and rely on it at times and you will eventually become a phenomenal intuitionist. Once you make an intuitive connection with a spirit, it is easy to keep the connection for future psychic work.

It is possible to connect with this realm more easily by practicing meditation, joining a dream group, recording dreams or working with an experienced psychic. However, the Spiritual Realm is most easily accessed after a loved one has passed away.

As an intuitionist, I have met several people who describe a sudden desire or impulse to have a psychic reading performed for them. They feel led to find answers to certain questions and by chance cross my path and sit down and have a conversation with me. They are not aware that a family spirit lingers in the door behind them and speaks to me throughout their reading. The spirit always gives good advice and loving concern.

Also, a spirit will attempt to contact you through the dream world. One example, I experienced was when a vivid dream accompanied by the voice of an older woman named Stella spoke to me. The voice attempted to contact me in the dream but at first I continued to sleep without paying much attention. And because I remained in a deep sleep, Stella used a signal that I would easily relate to, to get my attention. I continued sleeping until a loud telephone ringing sound voiced through the dream. Alarmed, in my dream state, I answered the ringing telephone and the woman's voice on the other end of the line spoke to me and told me that her name was Stella. I was tired and I wanted to go back to sleep. However, the prodding voice continued to persist and once again asked for me, sHEALy and now asked if I was the woman who could see into the future. At this time in my life I had been working with the public sharing intuitive information for approximately six years. This question got my attention because I was always looking for ways to improve my psychic abilities. Now that the voice had my attention it spoke louder and more clearly and gave me a message that has been with me until this very day. Stella's strong voice uttered that I had a destiny to share intuitive insights with people. Stella called me a visionary and told me to trust the spirit world. Most importantly, Stella told me to believe that my gift of intuition was real and loving and that I should continue to use it. She explained that I would some day save lives and souls. Then she, once again, identified herself by the name of Stella. I could see the older woman's face now as she spoke to me. She seemed relieved and her voice and face began to fade. I knew no one on this earthly realm named Stella and I did not know anyone who had passed into the spirit world named Stella either so I assumed Stella was just a friendly yet persistent spirit guide. Her image was gone, but I could still remember the image of the small boned, light skinned older woman.

The next morning when I woke I remembered the dream vividly. Like many spirit dreams, this one felt real and moving. I told a few people about the dream and believed immediately that the dream had been a sign of something to come. However, it was not until about a year later that I mentioned the name Stella to my mother while telling her for the first time about the dream. As I told her about the dream and its message encouraging me to continue my intuitive ventures, my mother casually mentioned that my great grandmother's name was Stella. I was surprised and knew immediately who the caller had been, my great grandmother. Although I had never met her, after doing a little family research, I was awed to find the small-boned woman smiling peacefully at me from a few old family photos. Stella is my great grandmother, although I had never met her, she found a way to contact me with information that is encouraging and helpful. Also, now my family has the satisfaction of knowing that Stella is still connected and watching over us.

Look into old family records if a spirit tries to connect with you. Usually the spirit can be found and it is someone who loves you. Yes, spirits loves you even though you have not met them yet.

Following the exercises provided below will help you discover the spirit realm and spirits who may be trying to speak with you. The exercise will guide you to relax and focus on your goals. Get ready to meet the spirit realm.

Spirit Exercises

1. Spend some part of your week meditating. You can do this alone or with a group. If you are meditating alone use the following meditation to enhance you spiritual clairvoyance. Tape-record your own voice using the meditation below. Play it while you are in bed at night or while you have a quiet moment in your day.

Spirit Ship Meditation

Close your eyes and breathe deeply....

Breathe in and out deeply....

See yourself seated on a comfortable boat.

You are warm and safe.

You are strapped into the boat and ready to enjoy yourself.

Breathe in and out deeply....

Relax and breathe....

Feel the boat begin to sway to the right and left.

Feel the gentle rocking of the boat.

Water flows below the boat. It is cool and refreshing.

Water flows below the boat. It is deep and dark.

Feel the boat gently rock right and left.

Feel the boat smoothly move forward.

You are safe and relaxed....

Breathe deeply....

As you move away from the shore. See the shore growing smaller and smaller. See yourself in the boat and the water around the boat moving faster now.

You are safe and comfortable....

Continue to breathe deeply and feel you arms growing relaxed and tired. Your shoulders are growing relaxed.

Your head and neck are tired and relaxed. Your eyes are closed and relaxed. Breathe....Breathe....Breathe....

The boat floats past trees and homes and busy cities but your eyes stay closed as if you are asleep. You are happy and willing to go on this adventure. You are at peace. You are calm and loved by the adventure in front of you. Breathe....Breathe....Breathe....Deeply....

See darkness and light mixed around your head. Your eyes are closed.

See darkness and light mixed around your body. Your eyes are closed.

See white light twisting around the boat and your entire body goes limp. Breathe....Breathe....Breathe....

Feel the boat rocking back and forward, back and forward. See the boat surrounded in light. White, Blue, Green, Red....

Feel the boat rocking back and forward, back and forward. See the boat surrounded in light. Yellow, Orange, Lavender....

The swirling colors are lifting the boat.

The boat is moving in a dream, into darkness, into light. The boat is filled with light and you.

See yourself. Your body is light. Your body is light.

See yourself. Your body is light. Your body is light.

The world......is gone......

The world......is gone......

There is nothing......

There is nothing......

You are approaching The Realm of Spirit

You see darkness......You see light......

Listen to the sounds.......

The Realm of Spirit is near.

Breathe....Breathe....Breathe....In......Out....

You are still, there is no movement, no time, all is forgotten, all is gone, you are in The Realm of Spirit.

Listen......

Breathe....

Spend time here with the spirits....listen....breath....listen......breath....listen....

2. Write a question to the realm of spirit on a piece of paper. Fold the paper and put it away in a safe place. Wait for the answer to come to you. You should see your answer come to you through a friend, a stranger, a phone call, even a television show. The answer might come to you in many different ways. Be open to hearing the answer to your questions and trust the answer when it comes to you.

3. Gather things that you love. Put them together in one small area of your home. This area should be used to inspire you and call spirit guides. You might want to place a photo of an animal that you like or a child that you love. You might find stones from a fresh garden or seashells from the sea. Try placing objects together in a colorful and whimsical manner. Add pieces of trees from the earth, scented candles for aroma, a chalice filled with salt water, a gold or silver coin, feathers you have found on the ground or herbs and dried flowers. This area will serve you when you need to feel nurtured or loved as well as call spirits closer to you. Place the objects near you when you need inspiration.

4. Find a token that represents your spirituality. You could select a goddess figure that represents strength or compassion. You could select an animal figure that represents your inner personality. You could select a crystal or mineral that represent special qualities.

5. Adopt an animal companion. Be aware that there is responsibility that goes along with this choice. The responsibility will be good for you. An animal, such as a dog or a cat, can transmit spiritual messages from the spirit world. If you spend time with an animal, you will learn his or her personality and be able to notice unusual behaviors when they appear. Because animals are very sensitive to spirit energies, your animal friend will help introduce you to the spirit world.

6. Spend time investigating objects that once belonged to someone who has passed into the spirit world. Selecting an artist or musician to study will be fun and interesting. If you chose to spend time with

the art works of Van Gough or the music of John Lennon you will be amazed when their spirit connects with you. Chose an artist or musician who you would like to connect with today.

7. Make a special friendship with a person who is about to move into the spirit world.

8. Dance and move your body. Movement will help you to experience a spirituality that is transmitted through the air and sky. When you dance do not concentrate on your appearance. Move to express your emotions. Stretch and leap into the air. Attempt to fly like an eagle or leap like a frog. Dance to the vibrations of life and you will be dancing with the spirits.

9. Listen to the sounds of the universe. The universe speaks with a high-toned voice; we hear it with our intuitive ears. First, find silence within a space without commotion. Intensely listen to the sounds of nature. Find your silent peaceful place either under a tree, in an open field or in your own backyard. At first you might hear frogs, crickets, birds, animals, people, city life, or other sounds, but eventually, you will learn to hear through all noise to hear only the high-toned hum of the universe. Attempt and practice this exercise often until you can hear the universal voice at will.

10. Face the south and give homage to the spirits of desire and passion. Southern energies are strongest in the summer months. They are filled with cleansing powers and passionate wishes. Honoring the power of fire will help you get in touch with south energies. Light a candle in honor of strength, power, passion, desire and warmth. Ask the energies of the south to visit your home and bring protection.

11. Collect stones from a running stream. Look for a smooth stone that has been brushed for many years by river water. A smooth stone will contain a spirit of memory. Keep this stone with you as you explore your memory and find spirits lingering there.

12. Linger in the spirit of contentment. Contentment will come to you when you have worked to achieve the things you desire. Contentment will cover you like a warm quilt. Work to achieve and find contentment today and you will know it always.

13. Walk between the worlds. Spirits live in this realm. It is unlike the earth we know. It is not a tangible place where physical matter exists. It is a place of love and psychic energies and divine contacts. To begin learning about this place, keep your intuitive eyes open and attempt to make contact with spirits in every possible way. Once you make contact, continue to speak to them and continue to be open to hearing their messages. Eventually, you will be invited to see with your intuitive eyes. As you become more familiar with this realm, you will learn to walk between the worlds in your dreams, your imagination, or with your intuitive vision.

Angelic Realm

The Angelic realm is filled with such beauty that humans can barely imagine it. It is filled with light, sound, energy and yes, angels, too. This realm is responsible for auras, angelic images, miracles, synchronicity, and beautiful clairvoyant visions available to those who are looking. This realm is most helpful when attempting to answer questions that are extremely important to the questioner. The energies found in this realm are much more than the typical angels that we have learned to expect from watching television shows and reading fairytales. These angels are more diverse and elaborate than most humans will ever imagine. In fact, these creatures are not necessarily angels at all. Yes, they are angelic but one would be tempted to categorize them differently if one could see or know them. Some of these beings are only voices. But, they are not voices like you and I have heard in every day life. In fact they are musical in nature. Imagine a bell tone or the wind blowing through tree leaves.

Imagine a baby breathing or a huge cold wave crashing on the beach and you will have heard the whisper of an angel's voice.

Some of these creatures are beings of light without bodily forms, while others reveal themselves in the shapes of rocks or tree stumps, burning fire or clouds. While some of these creatures have been caught in photos an intuitive eye most often views them. A mist of color or even a mood or feeling can suggest the presence of one of these creatures. They are quite lovely and powerful, but they have never been part of the human race. They seek love, divine happenings, joy, health, peace and serenity. But they are also quite fun and seek laughter and song, too. It is from this realm that one often gathers information truly needed to create a fun loving and satisfying life. It is unfortunate that some people do not desire to hear angelic messages, opting instead only to look into mundane matters. However, angels can and will answer mundane kinds of questions because it is these lessons that affect every humans' life. But it is divine happiness that the angel truly desires; everything else is just icing on the cake of life.

The angelic realm is available always and to everyone. You, the seeker, only need to ask. If you desire to connect with this realm, pray, write, ask out loud or before going to sleep at night meditate to this realm of energy. Ask for the angelic realm to visit you and it will. If you desire to see the beauty of auras begin your studies here at the angelic realm and you will someday find angels in every face that you meet.

You will enhance your daily life with the connection to this realm because you will always have the angelic energies watching over you. If you chose to make changes in your life you can be sure that the angels will see to it that you always move in the correct direction. They will help you to recognize that life is beautiful and loving.

You will discover that you are a visionary when you connect with this energy because you will be able to visualize anything that you desire and you will see the clear road to get to these desires. Others around you will notice that you have a special quality and they will want It, too. You will have the opportunity to share with others what you have learned; angels will make certain of this.

Visionaries, philosophers and enlightened public speakers draw energy from this realm. A popular public speaker once shared her experiences with me. She was scheduled to present a speech to a large audience, hoping to sway the group of listeners to give of their time and funds to a national charity. The speaker spent several hours preparing her speech researching demographics and the specific needs of the women and children who needed to receive help from this audience. She felt that she had a powerful oration, one that would definitely influence the group to get involved. She was ready and eager to meet the audience when she suddenly came down with an unexpected and unusual dose of stage fright. She tried to force herself to relax, but her fears only grew. She actually began to feel sick and thought about canceling when it dawned on her that her stage fright might be a signal from the angelic world. She had just recently begun working with the angelic realm with an intuitive reader; the reader had mentioned that angel energies sometimes take drastic measures to get one's attention. Immediately, the speaker stopped all action and asked the angelic realm for guidance at this difficult moment. Suddenly, she realized that she had forgotten to add an important piece of information to her speach; one that would help present just how desperately in need were the women and children. With that realization, her stage freight left her, turning into energy and excitement. Immediately, the speaker knew that she was going to present a great speech and get the job done well. She presented her speech and even added some on-the-spot insights thanks to the angelic world. Later that evening, the speaker received a phone call and celebrated earning more than two hundred thousand dollars for the charity.

If you choose to develop a relationship with the angel realm, practice the exercises below. They have been specifically created with the help of the angelic realm. Once you have opened the doorway into this realm you will never want to close it. Have fun and get ready to meet the angel world.

Angelic Exercises

1. Take 15 minutes each day to look at all of the beautiful colors around you.

2. Take 15 minutes each day to record all of the miracles that you can find around you. Remember that miracles are everywhere, the birth of a baby, the growing of a child, the blooming of a flower, love in a lover's heart, the wag of a dog's tail, rain, snow, nightfall, sunrise, sunset, breath, getting that new job, quitting that old job, making a new friend.

3. Begin to talk about angels with close friends. You will be surprised to hear about their experiences and beliefs.

4. Attempt to draw or paint faces or bodies of angels. Do not be ashamed or fearful of your artistic abilities. Let the spirit of the Angelic Realm flow through your heart and into your arm and out onto your paper.

5. Explore new aromas. Cook with scented seasonings, wear flowery perfumes, burn scented candles, bath in sweet scented bath oils, put lavender in your bedroom drawers, drink scented herbal teas, visit flower shops, picnic in an apple orchard.

6. Begin to sing. Your voice will improve and people will be attracted to your fun loving heart. You will discover that perfection is not needed.

7. Create an aroma that you love. Experiment with seasonings that can be bought at a local market or store. Blend them together until you find a scent that you love. Keep this scent on your body or in your house as a reminder that angelic energies are in the air.

8. Spend time bathing in angelic energies. Give yourself the royal treatment. Spend a few minutes in the shining sun. This is a good way to boost your immune system. Next, cleanse your body and

refresh yourself with a warm cup of herbal tea. Take a long bath in scented water and meditate as you soak your body in the warm water. Ask the angelic world to cleanse and fill you with sparkling angelic energies. Than take a long nap while listening to music you love. Wrap yourself in cool sheets while sleeping and stretch out and let the angelic energies enter your body.

9. Write poetry quickly. Do not stop to think about what you are writing. Do not be concerned about spelling or punctuation. Then go back and read the message that the angels have sent to you.

10. Watch the fall sky. Look at the stars and you will see them vibrate and breathe. Realize that you are connected to these stars by a magnificent life force.

11. Unclutter your work and living environment. As you clear clutter out of your life you will discover that your inner thoughts and emotions will become clearer as well. You will soon discover that you have space inside of your own mind to fill with angelic energies.

12. Write an incantation to the powers of the West. Western powers are strongest in the fall months. They give strength to the dream world, creativity, imagination and love. Stand facing the West and ask the western energies to visit your home bringing enjoyment and intuition.

13. Angels will attempt to teach you if you are open to their lessons. Watch for shapes to appear in shadows, clouds, tree trunks or any other natural object. Angels will attempt to present themselves to you in the physical form if this presentation helps you to learn. Take walks in nature with the intent of seeing angelic shapes. You will find that angelic shapes are not just winged creatures but, unicorn forms, animal forms, facial expressions, outlines of human shapes or any unusual shape that catches your eye. Look closely and try not to judge what your eyes see. Look with your intuitive vision and trust that you will find that which you seek.

Godly Realm

The Godly realm is the realm of your creator. It is here where the energies of all life begin and end. The Godly realm sets all creation in place and it gives continuous energy to our lives in the form of fate. It is here that you should check in when in need of nurturing or healing your past mistakes, and through prayer you can ask to act in accordance with your predestined fate. Although you can control much of your future, fate is still a part of life and you must combine the energies of fate and freewill to create the best life can offer. It is this place that great leaders look toward for guidance. Rabbis, priests, priestesses, heirophants, psychics and shamans come to this realm to learn and to gather power to teach and live. You can come here for guidance, too. Here, the greatest teachers of all time have come to acquire information. Here, those powerful teachers still exist today: Higher Power, Goddess, God and a universal energy.

When using your intuitive abilities you must be careful to work for the good of mankind. Ask this simple question and trust that the appropriate answer will come from The Godly realm. Ask; "What should I be doing today?" You will always receive the correct answer when asking this question. The correct action is not always the easiest or the fastest but it is always the best course of action to take. Attempt to make a connection with this realm each day and whenever in need of direction.

The Godly realm is always open to you. Respect and love this energy and you will begin to know yourself and your abilities with such insight that nothing will be impossible to you. You will be able to visualize all that your life is meant to be and all that you want it to be as well. You will make fewer mistakes when making decisions and you will develop long lasting relationships. You will understand any struggles that face you and gladly learn from them. You will be filled with such serenity that you will know that you are living each day to its fullest.

This realm wants you to experience a good life and you will begin to realize exactly how to do that. Because you are growing in inner knowledge, you will discover the true meaning of affluence and you will become an affluent individual and your prosperity will grow throughout your lifetime.

True, this realm will speak to you and tell you when you have fallen off course. You just need to learn to listen and see the signs. If you continue to use your intuition, you will notice small miracles appear around you on a regular basis.

One example of this happened to me years ago. My mother gave me a diamond ring. It was beautiful; set in white gold and perfect. Most important, however, was the fact that my mother had saved the ring for me for several years. She had eagerly awaited the day that I turned sixteen years old so that she could share the ring with me. When she gave me the ring, she gave it to me with a warning; "Do not lose this ring, whatever you do". I took the ring and was happy to wear it. Eventually I placed the ring safely in my jewelry box in the hopes of keeping it safe. After a few days my mother noticed that I had not been wearing the ring and she asked me about it. I was happy to share with her that the ring was in a safe place; upstairs in my jewelry box. I went up stairs and opened the box to get the ring and show it to her but did not expect what happened next. I looked through the entire box; under necklaces and other rings, but the ring was no place to be found. It was gone! Of course, I was upset and so was my mother. We searched everywhere in the house and eventually decided that the ring was nowhere to be found. We searched the trash, the carpet, in all the furniture, everywhere. We even searched the dirty filter of the vacuum cleaner. All the while I could not understand what had happened. I knew I had put the ring in my jewelry box. The relationship between my mother and myself, strained already from normal teenage, daughter and mother events, grew even more tense. Over the next few days, I grew depressed and felt confused and upset that the ring was missing and that my mother was angry with me, when a friend of mine suggested that I try something new.

Now, what happened next almost sounds too unreal to be true, but it is true; every word of it. A friend suggested to me to ask a saint to help me find the ring. She said, "Go into your house and pray to the saint who helps people find things. Ask him to help you locate the ring. It will work!" I went home later that day and sat on an outside bench near the location my mother was working. I just sat there feeling badly when my mother began to tell me about the ring. She told me that the ring was special to her only because it would eventually be handed down to me. She told me that there had been many times in her life when she could have sold the ring and used the money from the sale. She had been tempted to sell the ring but she could never bring herself to do that because she wanted to save the ring for me. She spoke and I listened and I grew to understand the importance of the ring. The ring was not a ring at all. The ring was a symbol of her love for me.

At that very moment, I felt something that a typical 16-year-old daughter is unable to feel. I emphasized with my mother and realized just how much I meant to her. For the first time, the little girl inside me was able to look at my mother through mature eyes. I learned a valuable lesson in that moment. I learned that my mother needed me to know that she loved me. She needed me to appreciate her and to recognize sacrifices she had made for me.

I felt overwhelmed and filled with an emotion that words can not explain. I got up and did just as my friend had suggested. I stepped into my house, through the back patio door, and began to pray. As I climbed the stairs to my bedroom, I felt that although I knew the ring was gone and would not be in my jewelry box, I just had to have faith and look again. I opened the box and my eyes saw something that they could not believe. The ring was lying right there in the little pink box, on top of all the other jewelry; just where I had left it and just where I had looked so many times. Tears filled my eyes and I ran down the stairs to my mother with the ring in my hand. I told her where I had found the ring and she looked at me amazed too. "I looked in that jewelry box too. I even dumped every thing out onto your bed and looked through all of the jewelry", she said.

That day the Godly realm taught me, and perhaps her too, a big lesson. Respect the love of those who love you and need you. I have never forgot that lesson. Working with the public, I have often seen similar situations where a piece of jewelry is lost. Pay attention to the signs around you if you lose a piece of jewelry. The Godly realm might be trying to tell you something. You might need to spend more time with a loved one, or appreciate someone, or understand something. Whatever the message, try to be open to the miracles of the Godly realm and it will help you realize what you need to know.

Although this realm often brings goodness into your life, it is true also that this realm can make something you are trying to achieve impossible, if you are not meant to be moving in that direction. You might wonder why you are struggling. You might wonder how to change a negative situation for the better. Soon enough however, you realize that the Godly realm is trying to guide you to go in a different direction. Perhaps you have landed a job that you love and think is perfect but suddenly you run into unexpected difficulties. You attempt to correct the problems and than go on with the job but soon afterward new difficulties occur. Again, you make changes and attempt to keep a positive perspective. But eventually you realize that the job you loved so much is too great a struggle and not what you expected. You intuit these difficulties as messages from the Godly realm. These messages are intended to tell you that you are not supposed to keep this job. You leave the job and feel blessed to have such a good connection with godly energies. You trust and love this realm and eventually find a better job.

The following exercises will aid you in connecting with this realm. You will be touched emotionally by these exercises. They will help you develop an intuitive connection to this divine realm.

Godly Exercises

1. Spend time with people who love you. Spending time with loved ones will help you to hear the voice of God because God often speaks through loved ones.

2. Give of your time to others in need. Find a charitable organization and spend time with people who need help finding their divine path. You will find good opportunities here to share your insights as well as your love. You will begin to share advice and your intuitive abilities will be enhanced as you do this. You will discover that your desire to help others is so strong that information from the Godly realm sometimes flows from your lips. You will learn to trust and continue to channel this type of information.

3. Give away what you do not need. You have negative energies around you if you are saving items that are unnecessary to your daily existence. When you free yourself from these physical items you will clear away old negative energies and open the door to new healing energies. God will help you create new situations when you clear out the old.

4. Ask Godly Energy daily to place you on the right path. Tell this energy everything you have ever desired and everything you desire today. Listen for a response from this energy. You will hear a response intuitively. Share all of your thoughts, hopes, desires, concerns, intentions and actions with this Godly Energy. Invite this energy to be your best friend and constant companion.

5. Listen to the wind. During the next storm find a quiet room and listen to the wind as it speaks spiritual messages to you. Your intuitive abilities will learn to listen to the voice of God.

6. Heal your home by performing a ritual of health and safety. Use Lavender incense, sea salt and water to perform the ritual. Place all of these objects next to your bed the night before you perform

the ritual. Ask the Godly realm to bless the objects and allow them to be used as healing tools. Sleep until you are rested. When you wake, begin the ritual by lighting the Lavender incense. Repeat these words as you light the incense. "East Air, South Fire, The desire to bind the healing we find." Now, begin in the eastern area of your home; walk around the entire room from corner to corner allowing the smoky air to fill all that you see. Continue until you have covered every area in your home, ending in the north. Repeat this incantation as you walk from the east to the north. "Through the powers of East and South, Air and Fire, Health and Safety I desire." When you have covered your entire home, go back to your bed and gather the sea salt and water. Mixing the sea salt and water, repeat these words. "West water, North land, the desire to bind the healing we find". When you have mixed the salt and sea together, begin again in the East are of your home. Walk from corner to corner sprinkling the sea salt and water as you repeat this incantation, "Through the powers of West water and North earth, call upon safety's birth." When you have completed this ritual you will be in the northern area of your home. Now, look to the north and complete the ritual with the following words. "By the powers of God and me, make this incantation be set free, to do no harm or cause no ill will. Bring safety and healing if you will". Your home is blessed.

7. Rethink your career goals. They must be in line with your life's purpose if you are to have happiness and a relationship with the Godly realm. Make a list of work opportunities that would better suit your needs. Hang up the list in a visible area of you home and think about it for a few days. You will soon begin to see other work opportunities come to you.

8. Write down on a sheet of paper the names of people who have harmed you. Title the list, "People I will forgive". Periodically chose a name from the list and spend a few days praying for this person. Ask the Godly realm to help this person find peace and

common sense. You will discover that you have moved closer to forgiving this person at the end of the week of prayers.

9. Stop holding back emotions. Begin to express your emotional aspects today. If you are angry, say so. If you are happy, say so. If you are sad or embarrassed, say so. You will begin to discover that the Godly realm often speaks to you through your emotions. Once you have begun to verbalize your emotions you will develop a more honest relationship with your inner self and the Godly realm.

10. Overcome old fears by sharing them with the Godly realm. Participate in a ritual to relieve your fears on a bright Sunday morning. Open your curtains and let bright light and sun shine into the room. Then begin to tell the Godly realm what you fear. You will find that the healing light is a gift able to melt away fears.

11. Release love into the Universe. Take several chances to share love with those around you. Send cards, write letters, make phone calls, make gifts or create your own method to release love to others. This exercise is important for you to perform as often as possible. You must strengthen your heart energy so that you can use this energy to receive Universal love. Your heart energy will grow stronger and more clear as you practice releasing love. Hug, laugh, cry, kiss, make love, eat good foods, listen to good music. Do everything you love and show love as much as possible. You will become a more loving person and your love of life will grow strong.

12. Stand facing the north and look for physical strength and health. With bare feet stand upon the earth and peer into mountain tops as you ask the north to bring health and wisdom into your life. Northern energies create strength, long life and reincarnation. These energies are strongest in the silent hours of winter.

13. Make a rock garden on the northern side of your home. Fill the garden with rocks of different sizes and colors. The garden will call upon the energies of knowledge and good health.

Magical Realm

The Magical realm is the most mystical of all the energies. This realm and all the other energies combined, can be available for your use. Here all of the energies merge into an eclectic sort of mix. This is the place where anything can happen. Very few individuals have mastered the use of the energies of this realm but those who have attempted, usually have great stories to tell. Here we find power animals, nature spirits, familiars, shape shifters, fairies and magic. This is the place our dreams sometimes visit when we are seeking change or adventure. This is the energy that is pliable. The Magical realm, like all of the other realms, is real, but requires a guided hand to enter its doorway. Magic is a tool to use for the good of mankind. Psychic abilities, healing, growing fruits and vegetables, raising children, loving each other, finding the love you desire, creating the life you want, talking to the angels and the spirits and living a full life, are all forms of magic.

Magic is the ability to change predetermined events. It is the ability to reshape one's life into a chosen destination. Using intuition wisely, you can produce a change in the course of your life. The possibilities of magic were first proven to me one night when I witnessed a life-changing event unfold before my eyes. I had started a dream group with a few friends. We met every Wednesday night, read our dreams to each other and ended the evening by performing a simple ritual. Each of us would take turns creating and leading her own ritual; usually creating simple chants, planting seeds in pots for prosperity or some other life affirming exercise. It was always fun but never too serious until one night when my friend, Vickie, suggested we attempt to perform a ritual that could possibly improve the life of a little girl. The group had been meeting for approximately three months and our energy was growing good and strong by now, so everyone agreed that our magic might possibly be powerful enough to create a real change in this little girl's life. This little girl, Michele, had several difficulties in her life and needed someone to intervene. She was now living alone with her dad and at times he was quite violent. After discussing what practical changes the community had attempted to make in the child's life we all agreed that magic might be the best resource to use. We planned and started our ritual, with Vickie leading us, first praying, chanting and than getting down to real business. We started by visualizing the little girl. We all attempted to see her and psychically connect to her, telling her that she would be safe and that people loved her. Than, holding hands we attempted to channel information that would help us make her safe. Eventually, we decided the best action to take was a positive one; instead of attempting to take the little girl away from her dad, we attempted to make positive changes in their lives. We set our minds toward making changes in Michele's adopted father's attitude. Apparently, Michele's adopted father was struggling to raise a nine-year-old daughter alone; he worked long hours and came home tired and irritable. He was uneducated as to how to raise a child and his patience was short. So, we began a ritual that would offer help and education to a man of his means. We poured a small bowl of milk and placed it between us on a table and repeated these words, "Mother's milk, Natural from thee. Mother's love. Go to thee". We chanted these words, over and over while visualizing a nurturing instinct filling the intuition of the adopted father. When we felt we had released all of the energy that was needed to complete this ritual we prayed and asked that this ritual cause no harm, only good. Vickie took the milk and placed it outside on my cement patio knowing that an animal would soon come from the woods and lap it up. Sure enough, about an hour later, the milk was gone. We celebrated knowing that nature, herself, was showing us that she was willing to help us. As the dream group ended that night we committed to spend the next week sending positive visualizations to Michele's father. Each night, I visualized Michele's father holding her and telling her that he loved her.

When we met the next week, Vickie told us that she had seen Michele playing outside of her house and that Michele appeared to be happier and more carefree but Michele's father looked sad and depressed. So again we performed magic, with Vickie leading us. We chanted and prayed hoping to see more of a change in the lives of these people. This evening Vickie brought silk material and tree limbs into the ritual. We worked together to make a beautiful and brightly colored kite for Michele. When it was finished we prayed over it and asked that Michele be happy and safe. We asked that Michele's father be kind and loving. That night, Vickie took the kite and placed it on Michele's front steps. A few days passed until Vickie saw Michele again. Tears filled my eyes when Vickie told the dream group what had happened. "The day was beautiful," she said "a gentle wind was blowing from the South; Michele and her Dad were outside together, both smiling and running down the street. I was surprised when I heard them laughing together, but I almost fell over when I looked up and saw that kite-the one we made-floating in the sky above their heads".

Since that occurrence, I have seen magic work several times but I will always be most grateful for that experience. It taught me that anything can happen or be changed if I only work to create the change.

You have created your life as it is now. Now, using your intuitive abilities and magic you can begin to bring into your life the changes that you desire. If you want to achieve anything at all, the magical realm is there to help you. Imagine you want to take a trip around the world. You have planned for this trip for two years but you still do not have enough money to seal your plans. Using a little homegrown magic you can help yourself find a way to set your plans in motion. First, sit back and organize your thoughts. Examine what you have done thus far to save and plan for this trip. Now, decide what you have left to do. If you have discovered that you are short of funds to go on this trip use your psychic abilities to call good energies toward you. Begin to visualize the trip. First see the your destination. Next, see what you will be wearing and where you will be staying. Visualize the weather and the company you will keep while on this trip. See everything, including the food you will eat, your suitcases, your means of travel, your hotel room, and see yourself celebrating and enjoying the trip. Now, spend a few nights visualizing this and meditating about the trip. Ask all of the energy realms to help you. Ask if the trip is good for you. If you receive a positive message then continue to visualize and ask the realms to help you intuit the best actions for you to take in order to accomplish the trip. Record your dreams and thoughts. Ask the magical realm to create a path for you to take to achieve your desires. You will soon discover that practical information will be sent to you. Perhaps you will receive in the mail information pertaining to discount airline tickets, or you might be suddenly offered a few months of overtime work. You might discover that a new destination is suddenly more attractive and much less expensive than your original destination, or you might realize that postponing your trip one more year will allow your best friend to accompany you as you travel, making your trip even more fun and exciting. Whatever the situation, the magical realm will offer practical advice and real action as well. By connecting to this realm you will find that you can create any positive circumstance that you desire to create.

The following exercises are created to get you on the path to working good magic. Have fun with them.

Magical Exercises

1. Plant a small section of corn and watch it grow. The natural growing cycle of the corn will teach you about the natural cycles of the seasons. You will learn when to begin new adventures, when to let things cultivate and grow and when to harvest the fruits of your desires.

2. Hike in the woods and watch for nature spirits. You will notice shapes in trees and rocks. You will notice unusual yet natural

visions. Nature spirits are a normal part of your existence. They exist everywhere and they deserve to be recognized and respected.

3. Go after what you know you love with a vengeance. Be powerful and positive about all things. Believe that you deserve to produce your desires.

4. Make a special place for your magical tools. This space should be safe and respected. No one should feel free to invade your special space.

5. Make magical tools. Fill silk and satin bags with scented herbs. Gather aromatic candles. Find and keep a special mirror that will show you your true beauty. Learn to love the image in the mirror. Look at it often.

6. Believe in magic.

7. As you experience magical circumstances continue to question, learn, and let magic teach you. Open your intuitive doorway to conversations with angels and spirits. Look for the presence of spiritual messages everywhere you go. Notice small creatures working and playing outside your home. Become intimate with the outdoors. Develop a loving relationship with nature. It will teach you always. Plant magical herbs and a small tree inside or outside. Watch them grow. Work to keep them alive and healthy. They will teach you magical secrets.

8. Become a magical herbalist.

The planting, growing and harvesting of certain herbs will enhance your relationship with the magical world. Following is a list of magical herbs and their attributes. They can easily be cultivated in your home. Chose at least one of these herbs to grow while developing your magical knowledge. You will begin to see positive changes in yourself as your knowledge grows. Enhancing your knowledge of magical herbs will help you develop new aspects of your character and lead you toward an affluent and knowledgeable group of individuals. Your life will begin to change for the better. You will notice definite and positive changes to your personality as you spend time growing magical herbs. Your intuition will continue to develop, your health and prosperity will increase and your desires will be realized if you dedicate yourself to this work.

After you have grown your first magical herb you may desire to share your new knowledge with others. Either share your information with friends or share the fruits of your herbs with friends. You may share cuttings from your herbs or products produced from the dried herb. However, be careful if you chose to give your herb plant away to a special friend. Make sure that the herb will be well loved and nurtured. When you are ready choose another herb and continue your learning process. Record all that you learn on the following pages.

Aloe—The Aloe will teach you independence. As the Aloe grows in your house you will notice this is a plant that does not like to be given too much water. This is a plant that does not like to be touched often. Although the Aloe plant has powerful medicine and can soothe pain, the Aloe likes to be left alone. As you watch the Aloe grow, you will begin to experience the power to make decisions and take new chances in life. You will begin to desire to seek a new and powerful direction for yourself without interference from others. Although you are loving, you will nurture your inner strength to be used when needed.

Basil—The basil plant will grow into a delicious kitchen helper. As you grow this herb you will find new ways to domesticate your skills. If you long to create positive domestic circumstances, grow and cook with Basil. Basil will teach you the joys of peaceful communications and the pleasantries of living with others in a home. Basil will help you to learn the skill of cooking as well as tempt a soul mate to spend extra time at home.

Dandelion—The Dandelion is so easy to grow but hard to send away. This herb will teach you to create a multitude of that which you desire. As you watch the dandelion grow you will notice that it seeds quickly and abundantly. It allows its seeds to blow in every direction. Most dandelion seeds are fertile and begin to sprout. Watching the dandelion, you will discover that you too have the ability to send many seeds into the world around you. You can begin many adventures and grasp many opportunities. You will begin to seek various adventures without fear of failing.

_____

_____

_____

_____

_____

_____

_____

_____

_____

_____

_____

_____

_____

_____

_____

_____

_____

_____

_____

_____

Honeysuckle—Honeysuckle can be grown in your back yard or in a large outdoor pot. Honeysuckle offers an attractive aroma. Honeysuckle attracts many insects as well as humans with its sweet fragrance. If you grow Honeysuckle you will quickly learn the secrets of quietly attracting visitors with your special gifts. You will begin to place extra emphasis upon your unique qualities until they have grown to fulfillment. Growing honeysuckle around your home wards off loneliness. If you desire a life filled with more visitors and friends, plant honeysuckle and learn.

Lavender—Lavender is filled with its own brand of beauty. Lavender brings beauty into every home. Lavender is filled with its unique brand of fragrance as well. If you desire to be a unique individual, learn from the Lavender herb. Lavender does not let any other plant steel its beauty or fragrance. Lavender is willing to last a long time and can be used to freshen any room in your home. Lavender's magical properties are many. Lavender, when placed next to you bed or pillow at night, will enhance your dreams. Lavender will encourage the growth of intuition and clairvoyant abilities. Lavender is the favorite herb of magical herbalists. If you chose to share its gifts with your special friends, plant Lavender in your home. Lavender will allow you the opportunity to nurture and keep your friendships, as well as help you to develop into an enchanting individual with much to give others.

Marigold—Marigold grows with the strength of a weed, yet its beauty soars in the hot summer air. Marigold holds its color and strength when others around are withering from the heat. If you desire to keep strong when others are at their weakest, draw strength from Marigold. The Marigold was named because of it's beautiful golden and red-hot color. Plant plenty of Marigold seeds at your backdoor and you will find that you can accomplish any feat. When Marigold returns the next Summer, your abilities will grow in strength.

Mint—Mint is a friendly herb. Mint will visit every house in the neighborhood, if you allow it to continue it's path. If you chose to discover new avenues of experience and have more adventure, make friends with Mint. It comes in so many varieties you will not know which to choose first. If you want to plant firm roots and stay in a home forever, plant Mint.

_____

_____

_____

_____

_____

_____

_____

_____

_____

_____

_____

_____

_____

_____

_____

_____

_____

_____

_____

_____

_____

_____

_____

_____

_____

_____

Rose—Ahh, what beauty, what aroma, what magic is here? Rose is the flower of Queens. If you want a special romance to bloom, bring fresh cut Rose into your home. Keep the aroma around you and you will develop the knowledge of Rose. Rose attracts love and admirers. Rose is honored and respected. Call respect, honor and love to your life by planting Rose.

Tea—Tea builds strong teeth and attracts good health. Tea comes in many colors and flavors but it is the green leaf that magically creates health. Enjoy a warm or cold cup of Tea each day and you will discover new and improved health. Anti-aging effects will come from Green Tea, so, if you desire to live a long long life, enjoy Green Tea every day.

Wild Strawberry—Wild Strawberry is nature's food. It attracts nature's creatures because it can offer a home and nutrition as well. If you think you are interested in honing your skills, allow Wild Strawberry to grow near your front door. Wild Strawberry grows quickly and easily, attracting good luck and a multitude of opportunities. You will love its attractive appearance and you will enjoy the creatures that come to visit when Strawberry grows near your home.

_____
_____
_____
_____
_____
_____
_____
_____
_____
_____
_____
_____
_____
_____
_____
_____
_____
_____
_____
_____

9. Repeat the following incantation when you desire something: Earth, Air, Fire and Sea; with your powers I desire to see. Earth, Air, Fire and Sea, this desire come to me. Earth, Air, Fire, Sea, with your powers I desire to see. Earth, Air, Fire and Sea, this desire come to me.

10. Spend time with the four elements of the Universe, Earth, Air, Fire and Sea. Learn and develop a special relationship with each. Use fire to help warm your home. Allow air to flow freely through your home. Bring earth inside your home by growing plants. Bring water into your home with a fish tank or a fountain.

11. Face the East and ask for fertility. Eastern energies are strongest in the Spring months. They bring new beginnings and inspiration.

12. Plan a Spring garden on the Eastern side of your home. The garden will bloom in the Spring, rejuvenating your intuitive abilities.

13. Pray to the God of your choice, each day.

Now that you have worked through the exercises in this chapter you will find that it is possible to integrate some of the exercises into your daily routine. When you make even small changes in your daily routine, your attitude changes. If you have put effort into developing relationships with the five realms, undoubtedly you are beginning to feel different already; like a breezy Spring day, insight and the spirit of serenity are whisking over you. You will soon begin to experience the world in a different way, and you will begin to make constructive changes in your life as a result of your experiences. You will continue to use the energies available to you, along with your new found intuition, to enhance each day. As you move toward your next quest your life will feel like a beautiful dream where everything is possible. Keep working to improve your psychic abilities and all of your dreams will come true.

You are a magical spirit!

Part Two

Chapter Two

Soul Mate

It's time to find a soul mate. You have attempted to find your soul mate many times. You have tried many avenues but they have all lead to the same results; disappointment. Make today a memorable day. Make changes and do things differently, all in the name of finding your soul mate. You don't have to find your soul mate immediately. You have waited this long. Take the time to prepare yourself mentally for the meeting of this wonderful and loving person. Continue to work toward developing you inner strengths and your soul mate will come to you easily. You will travel in the right places and at the right times to begin wonderful relationships. Begin now to use your intuition to recognize your own needs and your soul mate will soon follow.

Life is to be lived in a complete and happy manner. A happy life is the best you can hope to achieve. One of the things necessary to developing a happy life is loving relationships. There are many kinds of relationships, but today we are going to focus upon the soul mate relationship. You will begin by developing a psychic connection to your inner self, and than eventually, your soul mate. This is not difficult to do. Read through this chapter and practice the exercises provided. You will learn three types of psychic communications: clear vision, clear hearing and clear knowing. Using clear vision, clear hearing and clear knowing you will find your soul mate with ease.

Clear vision

First you will use clear vision to prepare yourself for the adventure of discovering your inner soul and eventually finding your soul mate.

Clear vision is the ability to see circumstances that others do not see and with clear vision you can see the intentions, feelings, desires, hopes, fears, memories and disappointments of individuals that you meet. It is easy to develop this vision. First practice meeting new people. Visit a nearby county or town. Spend a portion of your day just watching the actions and activities of others. Becoming a people watcher is a fun hobby and it will help you to begin to recognize personal elements that are recognizable in all human beings. You will quickly begin to notice that certain individuals carry their bodies differently from others. Some use their bodies to send messages to others. For example, you will notice that some people send messages that call others closer while others send body messages that tell others to stay away. Watch for body language and begin to decipher what messages you receive. After a while, begin to imagine the personal lives of the individuals you are watching. Imagine the type of job each person has or imagine the home life each person is living. Try to intuitively decide who is friendly, who is busy, who is talkative and who is shy. After a while test yourself. Begin to speak to some of these individuals when you feel comfortable. Discover if your first impressions remain the same or are changed. With a little practice you will begin to be very good at reading other people. You will learn to read body language and personality types. You can use this information to chose the friendships that you make, and to recognize the signals that you are sending out to others. If you do not like what your body is saying to others, change it. Make you body begin to express respect, love and health. You will get these things back in return.

Clear Hearing

Listen for tones in voices when you speak to people. Eventually, you will develop clear hearing abilities. The human voice will contain many signals telling you many things about an individual. Speak to people and listen to the tone in their voices instead of what words they are actually speaking. A good way to practice clear hearing skills is over the telephone. When you speak to an individual over the phone, practice listening to tones in the voice. Listen for tones rising and falling as the individual speaks. Eventually, your intuitive abilities will awaken and you will develop the ability to hear what others cannot. After some practice, you will learn to know others from an intuitive perspective. You will recognize tones that are honest and friendly and tones that seem dishonest and afraid. You will be able to use this ability along with clear vision ability to chose your friendships. You can make changes to the tones in your voice too. You can develop a friendly tone of voice that calls for healthy love and respect.

Clear Knowing

You will eventually learn to hear and see angelic and spirit presences as you continue working toward psychic communications. As you grow you will develop a psychic ability referred to as clear knowing. Clear knowing is a fruit from the trees of clear vision and clear hearing. When you have honed your intuitive skills you will know yourself intrinsically and you will have the ability to make the best decisions and take the best opportunities life has to offer. Your soul mate will come to you easily when you have developed this skill because you will know where you belong in this life and you will know what you are to do to create the happiness that you desire. You will know the right things to do and you will do them.

A "clairgnostic"—a term I've coined—is an individual who knows the soul intuitively, psychically, spiritually and deeply. You will develop a gnostic perspective on life and begin creating friendships that are perfectly matched for you. Among these new relationships your soul mate will be waiting.

When you meet your soul mate you will know it. You will practice clear vision automatically and on a daily basis. And, using your clear vision abilities, you will see your soul mate and realize that this person is a good person with compatible attitudes and desires. At first, using clear vision will feel like a memory. You will not actually need to see with your eyes but with your heart and imagination. You will see someone new and have the sudden feeling that you have already met. You might even search your memory to recall a past meeting but than you will realize that it has not yet happened. You will realized that your clear vision abilities are simply allowing you to see that this person is right for you or that your future will be happy and complete with this person. Eventually, you will realize that clear vision feels like a memory.

When you remember the events of yesterday you visualize it in you mind's eye. Your clear vision will work in the same way. You will begin to see things with your mind's eye. You can close your eyes and see or you can look with your eyes open and see. But, you will know a good relationship when it comes to you.

You will inevitably make changes in the way you meet individuals. You will become more aware of your own body and voice image. When you begin to feel really comfortable with yourself, begin again to look at people who pass you on the street. Make eye contact now. If you have not been using your clairvoyant abilities for long you must at first begin to look for expressions and impressions. Once you have become more experienced using your clairvoyant sight you will sometimes see actual colors or light or even animal or spiritual guides around individuals you meet. Color will look like a thick mist that appears from parts of the body and than quickly fades. Spirits will look like faces and expressions reflecting from the faces of the individuals with whom you are attempting to connect. You will look into the face of an individual and see the big innocent eyes of a deer or the cunning smile of a fox. You will see the deep lines of an elderly Native American or the understanding expression of a Spiritual teacher or student. The faces of human and animal spirit will begin to look you in the eye when you truly have made the decision to pursue information using clear vision. Your clear vision will become more adept as time passes and you continue exercising it. Look into the faces of others and begin to notice the first impression that the individual sends to you. Soon, you will be able to do more than imagine the lives of these people who pass you on the street. You will begin to intuitively know their home lives and their families.

After a while, you will want to take the next step toward meeting new people. Begin to say hello to the people you pass. Say hello while intuiting whom the individual is and what the individual likes to do. You will begin to notice rather quickly that your psychic communications grow into images. You will begin, after a short time period, to see images around any person you choose to focus upon. Some of the images will be simple while others will be unusual. Do not judge the images. Continue to see them and spend a few minutes thinking about what you have seen. Remember, when you say hello to people you pass you will listen to tones and impressions in the voices. Eventually, clear hearing will develop into a deep connection to the intuitive world. You will sometimes hear thoughts of other human beings. You will sometimes hear messages telling you what you need to know. This will happen to you only if you are not afraid and only if you desire and pursue the knowledge that clear hearing can bring to you.

While practicing these methods you will develop a new group of friendships. You will integrate these practices into your daily life and you will find yourself growing happier yet anxious to go to the next step of finding a soul mate. In fact, your anxiety is a form of intuition. You are beginning to get close to your soul mate.

Clear hearing and clear vision often first present themselves through dreams. While dreaming you are trusting and free from judgments and fears that constrict your intuitive abilities. You can hear messages from spirits, angels and other human beings in the dream world. As you work through this book you will begin to record your dreams; make special notations of dreams that contain clear hearing messages. As you record your dreams underline messages that have been spoken to you or visions that seem important. These messages are encouraging you to find the life of your desires. Your soul mate will often speak to you through these messages and undoubtedly will be seeking your presence also.

You probably will discover that your soul mate is attempting to make a connection with you today. Your dreams will often reveal these important messages from your soul mate. It is possible to enjoy your soul mate today through your intuitive abilities and your dreams even though you have not met. If you want to connect with your soul mate through the dream world simply ask the dream world to help you. Before you go to sleep each night repeat a simple ritual. Light a candle and pray or meditate. Look into your inner vision and attempt to see your soul mate. After you have put out the burning candle, go to sleep. Repeat this until you have remembered your dream and gotten a glimpse of your soul mate.

Also, spend time each day developing both your clear vision and you clear hearing and you will be on the path to being a person you can admire, appreciate and love. Clear knowing will follow and continue to develop, too. Clear knowing comes from knowing yourself and using your intuitive abilities. When you have begun to develop your intuitive abilities you will notice that you can easily make decisions. You will more easily develop friendships and set healthy goals. You will let go of much of the fear that binds you. You will release the fear of the unknown and you will embrace new experiences. You will easily begin to set goals that will change your life and you will eventually find all that you desire. Your soul mate is one of the most pleasurable aspects of your life and you are not meant to live a life without finding at least one special person with whom to share your most intimate thoughts. Some people have been lucky enough to find several soul mates throughout their life times. Sometimes they come and go, but there is always the possibility of finding love again.

People who have followed their dreams are the happiest and live a fuller and healthier lifestyle. You can be one of these people by following the exercises in this manuscript and by learning to live using your intuitions. Your soul mate is an individual who has learned to do the same. Together you will know what life has to offer you. Together you will find each other and you will begin to make a life that is magical and real. You will develop a spirituality that compliments each other, careers that compliment each other and love that supports your special goals and ambitions. I know a wonderful woman, Donna, who followed an intuitive path and created a love life the like of which many only dream. She left a bad marriage and started a beautiful life with her soul mate only two months later. They are married, and living happily today.

The process of change she went through was not easy at first but grew easier as she grew to trust herself. I first met Donna 10 years ago when she came to me to have an intuitive reading. I recognized immediately that she loved and needed her husband very much but her emotions were not reciprocated. Like many men, her husband had not learned to use his emotions wisely. He was cold and unable to share love with her or anyone else. I urged Donna to see the good within herself and to create positive circumstances in her life. Together we worked to find ways to create the love that she needed and wanted; sometimes with good results but usually the psychic message that both of us received was clear; Donna would be happier if she left the marriage. Her husband had a heart of ice, there was no helping him. Donna was committed and honest to the relationship, attempting every strategy to create the love that she wanted within her marriage to no avail. Only after years of hurt and neglect did Donna finally allow herself to see that she was wasting her love and affections. By this time, Donna and I had developed a close relationship and became friends. I continued to perform intuitive readings for her and I watched her grow to trust her own inner voice. Donna, an intuitive young woman with a heart filled with affection and bursting with love was literally dying to love and be loved and eventually she made the only possible decision, she decided to let go of a marriage that had never embraced her. What happened next was pure magic. Donna quickly met a man who seemed too-good-to-be-true. But, he was true. Donna had made the decision to overcome her fears and to listen to the intuitive voice that had been shouting at her for years, and within days of making the final decision to leave the marriage Donna came upon the caring and loving soul of Mario. Mario, too was in a relationship that was filled with problems and neglect. He was unhappy and feeling stagnant. Life had lost all meaning for him, but he was looking for something more. The two paths crossed and Donna and Mario recognized each other immediately. They were like one in thought and heart. Their minds seemed to think the same and they grew aware of a connection that was more than usual. They were soul mates and they had found each other. It was time for them to trust their instincts and do what felt natural. This is often the time when individuals become so filled with fear that they become stagnant and stop using their intuitive knowledge. They stop moving toward the direction of love and they simply let it slip through their fingertips. But, Mario and Donna did not do this. They each made the commitment to begin a life together. There was much work to do and responsibilities to meet, but they worked through these obstacles and finally were free to begin their life. Like magic, both of their lives began to change for the better. Family and friends embraced them and filled their new home. Financial opportunities opened up to them as they continued to grow in love and spirituality. Their original intuitive vision had been correct. They were in love and indeed soul mates. Today they are living in a beautiful home on a hillside in a safe and prosperous community. They have the time and freedom to travel and enjoy life. They celebrate their relationship often and regularly entertain company and friends. Donna has found a poetic voice to express the struggles she once endured and today she spends much of her time allowing her intuitive voice to speak through poetry celebrating the joy and love she has found. She is one of the lucky ones. You can be too.

Practice the following exercises to develop clear knowing and find your soul mate.

1. Write to your soul mate as if you are connected today. Reveal your most private thoughts and desires.

2. Make an effort to communicate with at least one new person each day. Make the effort to go to new destinations to find new people with whom to converse.

3. Create a special area in your home where you and your soul mate will spend the most time with each other.

4. Create an advertisement displaying your unique qualities. Although it is not necessary to send this advertisement to a dating service it might be fun to peruse the dating service advertisements. Today electronic services have made finding a mate quite easy.

5. On a new moon, be bold and ask a potential partner to lunch.

6. Use the following pages to record intuitive thoughts, images and dreams you would like to share with your soul mate.

7. The following exercise, Recovery, Release and Rescue, is a collection of poems written by an intuitive and magical woman. Find a silent and peaceful space where you will not be disturbed. Read over the poems and allow them to move your emotions. They are created to help you release old pain and memories, improve your present circumstances and attract magical love to your future.

LIFE IS CALLING

I've reached
    my breaking point
exhausted
    from the emotions…
I can no longer be
    your once-in-awhile love
sustained by stolen
      moments…
occasional opportunities
for intimacy

The doors won't close
    by my hand
but I won't watch obsessively
for you to walk
    back through

Don't talk to me
about "processes"
I'm in enough pain
I cannot shadowbox
    with the struggles
      of your soul

You asked for time
    …fair enough,
    use it wisely
in the meantime
I will be kind
    to myself

...life is calling...
I defy sadness
      to overcome
      my spirit.

TRAGIC HEROINE

There is no honor
in being
      a tragic heroine
there's little comfort
in having the world
attest to
      a man's misjudgment
at denying an offering
      of love.

I want the affection
direct from the source
not messages
      sent through channels
I don't want to be
the girl he'd marry
if he was ready
      to fall in love

I want today...
not a gamble
      on tomorrow
there's no reward
for martyrdom
      ...no honor in being
      a tragic heroine.

TELL HIM GOODBYE

There's a point
    of surrender.

A time when you realize
you've backed yourself
    into a corner
        ...trapped yourself
        in a no-win situation
        ...lost control,
        sacrificed freedom...

If you're smart
you'll admit it's time
    to sell out
        ...total your losses
        and move on...
find the voice
    to tell him
to find someone else
to share his bed
    and his sorrows

After all,
    you can only
take so much
and already
    you've suffered
more then you should.

Tell him goodbye.

SOPRANO POSSIBILITIES

I strive toward
    soprano possibilities
open doors and windows
    …an abundance of light

I send my wishes
    traveling on the wind
vocalizing
    To higher octaves
refusing to settle
    into safe or comfortable
        ranges
risking…challenging
    stretching…
in order to reach
    an elevated awareness
the rewards
    and promises of life
    …the magic of it's
    melody…

CHILDHOOD FEARS
INTERFERE WITH A
GROWN WOMAN'S LIFE

There are issues
that ignite me
…not from a
present position
but a sensitivity

from the pain
of my past

Emotions interfere
so dramatically
from our rational thinking
…it can make
a minor inconvenience
seem overwhelming

fears can keep us frozen
and
distance can destroy us
…the fluidity of
our love is what's
so special…we must
protect it

When the frightened child
within me
cries in illogical terror
hold her tightly
…comfort her
with your caring
and she will go
calmly and silently
to sleep.

PEACE OFFERING

I found it amusing
that at first

when we…
you were on the defensive
…as if you'd spent days
preparing your opening
       remarks…

I wanted to assure you
that you were free
       to relax…
I didn't come
to beg you to love me
       or to question
              your motives.

The timing was convenient
so I stopped to share
       some conversation
and pick up the things
       I'd left behind.

It was a peace offering.

TRAITOR

You betrayed me.

With declarations
of innocence
and tales of injustice
you enlisted me
to go to war with you
…everyday…

side
    by
        side
we fought your battles
...I gave you pep talks
and dressed your wounds.

At night
you snuck into
the enemy camp
and slept with
the opposition

You are the worst
of traitors.

A GRADUATION

Did you think
I'd leave quietly
this time...
let you have
the last word?
...that was
before...when
I was
    a freshman
and respected
rank
...but
education
is cumulative

and I've learned
to defend myself
against attack…
I won't be dwarfed
by your aggressiveness
…you taught me well.

This is a graduation.

TEARS

It's too
Damn bad
That you
Can't stand
To see me
Cry…

You
Demanded passion
When it catered to you
And your physical
Male needs

Well honey,
        Tears
        Are passion, too
…it's the other
        extreme…

If I can
Stand to cry

Then you can
Stand to watch

By the way,
Who amongst us
Is exhibiting
A weakness?

…the one who
dared to feel
with intensity
or the man
who feared
the consequence
of feeling.

THE LAST, LAST CHANCE

Emotions
        Can arm-wrestle
                Reason
9-out-of-10 times
and regardless of
        the declarations
or threats we issue
most of us
        learn the hard way
…take the long way
home…
before we're able to
        stand behind our
                decree

...contemplate and
    execute
the last,
    last chance.

BANKRUPT

My heart has filed Chapter 11.

It needs
a major reorganization
in it's thinking.

I've set myself up
for too many failures
by leading crusades
for selfish lovers.

My expenses (pain)
Greatly exceed my income (love)

I feel bankrupt.

FIND YOURSELF A NEW SANCTUARY

I'm tired of
    sheltering you
    ...seducing you
sacrificing my sanity
    in pursuit of you

Find yourself
        a new sanctuary.

PUBLIC FACE

"Rule #1...
        keep your head
                up high"

Her mother
        taught her to be
                a survivor

Her father
        told her to
                be strong

In the privacy
        of her own home
                she cries.

YOU FOR ME

I wonder if you
        Could be
                For me...

It's hard to tell
By the resources
At hand
...the color
of your eyes

and the size
of your arms...

Even with
Such sketchy information
There's a
    Certain amount
        Of intrigue
...you've caught
my attention...

I could entertain
A romantic fantasy...

I wonder if I
    could be
        for you?

FRIDAY'S CHILD

My heart
    Was an orphan...

Aimless
    Wandering
        Lonely

...till you
    came along
        and offered
            me shelter...

you make me
    feel loved
significant
    ...special

Will you, my hero,
    Adopt me...
Give me
    a home
forever,
    for keeps?

LITTLE PISCES MOON

I will bring sunshine
into your life,
my little pisces moon,"

he whispered to me
as I smiled,
slightly self conscious
by the unfamiliar
gestures of affection
(I always wanted
    to be adored)

"But...
    But...
        But..."
I interrupted
(It had to be said)

"How long can
    this go on?
How far will we dare
    To take it?"
(Is it *always* our privilege
    to follow our passions?)

"Day by day,"
    he counseled
"let's take it
    day by day…"

NO FEAR, NO LIMITS

"No fear. No limits.
Really think
    About it…are you
    Ready for all this?"
        He demanded
All the while
    Holding my hands
        Tightly in his,
Never losing focus
    With my eyes.

"I don't do
    anything easy."
        He emphasized
…a point he didn't
    need to drive home.

After all,
    it was his intensity
    that first attracted me…
his pure and uncontained
    passion for everything
            in life
I responded to
    so strongly

"I'm with you…"
    I whispered
in response
    to his proposal

"I'm with you
    all the way."

MY BLESSING

You are my bright
    and dependable star
in a universe of
    uncertainty

There is safety
in an emotional expose
…I share with you
every feeling…every fear

you heal my heart
with acceptance and humor
and calm me
    with your commitment

You adore and assure me
…it is everything
    I've always needed
the one aspect that
eluded me for so long.

It is not everyday
    that we have
    the fortitude
to fight for our own
    best interests
acquiescing is easy…
It became an art form for me

But…
for one brave
and intense moment
I defined, for myself
the canvas of my future
and I have been blessed
immensely
    ever since.

WHAT I WISHED FOR

It's not everyday
    that when we get
        what we wished for
it's what we really want.

I am lucky.

Often
        the package's presentation
        evokes more emotion
                and desire
than the substance
        of it's contents.

Not this time.

I believe I am part
of a fortunate few...
blessed to have all of it
        through my love
                with you...
a best friend, a lover
        a true
dream come true.

8. Begin to love your body. You send unconscious signals through
   psychic channels to everyone you meet. If you love your body,
   your soul mate will love it also. Accept each crevice and curve.
   Explore every smooth surface. Look at yourself in the mirror and
   tell yourself that your are beautiful and that you deserve love and
   affection. Your soul mate will love you and your body when you
   love yourself and your body.

9. Read and visualize your soul mate.

Breath,	humid upon my neck
Smell,	thick and sweet
Arms,	strong and secure
Hair,	soft, silk, coarse
Eyes,	piercing

Embrace,	hard, tight, forever
Love,	real, safe and warm
Sex,	good, hot and loving
Taste,	salty upon my tongue and lips

10. Use your intuition to chose a date of fun and adventure. Take off from regular work. Buy a map and find a near-by city to visit. Allow your intuition to make most of the choices, today. Eat, shop, visit, sit, watch local folks and have fun. When the day is over, you will have broadened you horizons. Visit this city often and use your psychic abilities to make new friends.

11. Light a candle while facing the West. Repeat this incantation to call upon your psychic abilities and soul mate.

"Powers of the West, greatest passions of deep seas; fill my life, my home, my heart with passions. Western waters and sea of dreams, Water nymph, Coral God, Sea magic, waves; wash over me. Fill me. Sea of dreams, magic, psychic world, cast me into your soul. Sea of souls, I drift toward you with never ending desires of love". Embrace me, Soul Mate. Find me. Find me.

12. Imagine making love.

13. Smile at everyone you meet. When you smile you send a message to your brain that you are happy and content. Allow your smile to heal your past and send you into the world with positive energy. Your soul mate is on the way. Smile and be happy about that.

You are on the path to creating the love of your life. Your love life will soon to feel like a beautiful and magical dream. Keep believing in all that you want and you will keep love alive forever. You are now ready to move into the world of prosperity and onto your next adventure with your intuition strong and your love life secure. Keep going and you will have all that you can imagine.

You are filled with light and love!

Chapter Three

Creating Prosperity

Three Part One-as channeled from the realm of thought

You deserve to prosper in all that you do. Begin to believe in prosperity and it will come to you. The ability to be affluent; to have good friends, money, love and a happy life, is all you need in this lifetime. It is all anyone needs. Do you have everything of which you dream. If not, you will soon develop the ability to obtain your life's desires as you read and practice the recommended exercises found in this manuscript. You will first begin to change your attitude and the way you think about prosperity. You will begin to recognize that you have the abilities to claim opulence for yourself. When you recognize that affluence is more than just a filled bank account you will undoubtedly be able to recognize an ocean of affluence available to you today. Because prosperity is simply the ability to create opportunities and to be happy with the results of these opportunities, you can begin today to create affluence for yourself right now by claiming your own abundance. Use your intuitive abilities to recognize prosperity in your future activities. What activities do you see yourself pursuing? How do others relate to you as you claim your prosperity. How does your life change? As you visualize your future with additional prosperity, what specific changes do you see? Do you have better health, are you more attractive, do you have more financial power and closer friendships?

Now ask yourself what changes you can create today to bring all of these things into your life.

Now that you have used your intuition to see future prosperity, begin to make the necessary changes that are needed to create the prosperity that you desire. You might feel the need to develop relationships with a more affluent set of friends or you might decide to spend spare time in a variety of new locations. You could possibly decide that your wardrobe is in need of refurbishing and that you would like to change your outer appearance. As you grow and change internally you will crave outer changes as well. Both your inner attitude and your outer appearance will attract the type of prosperity you desire.

As you strive to create the type of affluence that feels comfortable for you, you will need to dive deeper into your intuition. You can dive deeper into your intuition by working with your dreams. As you pursue the life of your dreams, you will begin to make affluent decisions. You will find the intellect and strength to set positive goals and you will work toward the actualization of these goals. Simply ask your dreams to help you discover information. Ask your dreams to show you what you need and want from life and how you can best acquire these things. Your dreams will answer you by showing you symbols that will direct you toward affluence. Listen to your dream symbols and allow them to guide you. If you find yourself dreaming of a pleasant area of town, attempt to find that location and visit there with friends. If your dreams show you a frightening aspect of your life, attempt to make changes there, too. Over time, you will begin to recognize and work with your dream symbols with a newly acquired expertise.

As you continue to work with your dreams you can simultaneously work with visualization. Visualization is a phenomenal way to create prosperity. First, begin to visualize a new home. Imagine coming home to the house of your dreams. You comfortably climb into a warm bath and listen to relaxing music. While relaxing, you think about the events of the day and plan a night of pleasure. You have hired a band to play your favorite music while you entertain a few friends. You can smell the aroma of a scrumptious dinner cooking in the oven. You are confident that the evening will be fun and relaxing. You don't have a worry in the world.

Or, perhaps your dream life is more of an adventure; imagine hiking up a dense forest-covered mountain. You have been hiking for three months and you are having the most exciting adventure you have ever imagined. You have planned to be met at the top of the mountain by your privately owned helicopter. You will rest for one week at a local camp ground and than be flown to a private island of your choice. You love your life and you are happy to be alive.

Since most individuals desire only a simple life, your dreams of prosperity might contain only a bank account big enough to pay your bills, or a career that will allow you to take a vacation once a year. You might only desire to have a new car or an attractive wardrobe. Your dreams of prosperity might include enough money to pay a college debt or to buy a comfortable home in which to live. It is up to you to set your goals of prosperity. Anything is possible when you begin to recreate your life. Follow your dreams and set goals that will lead you toward happiness and an affluent life.

You have begun to attract an abundance of new opportunity with the onset of reading this book. As you continue to work through this chapter you will begin to use your intuition to bring the prosperity that you desire. Follow the exercises provided below and you will begin to see rich opportunities available to you.

1. Make a list of 10 objects you desire to own.

2. Pick one of the 10 objects you have listed and decide to make this a goal.

3. Share your desires with friends, family and new people you meet.

4. Pray and ask God and the spirit world to give you guidance in obtaining the goal.

5. Open a new and special savings account in which money will be saved for this object. Trust in the process.

6. Using your intuitive abilities, meditate upon opportunities that will help you achieve this goal. Ask during meditation how you might most quickly and naturally achieve this goal.

7. As you continue with the above exercises, begin to make a list of positive aspects of your life. This list will include friends, family and the pleasures of life. This list should include everything for which you are grateful. Read this list often. This list will help you recognize the present day prosperity that is available to you.

8. Set a goal to meet new people often. When you are working, shopping, traveling or relaxing, take the opportunity to speak to new people. Begin with saying a friendly hello, but practice light conversation as well. Soon you will intuitively know when a new friendship is becoming available. As you develop new friendships, new adventures and opportunities will present themselves.

9. Fill a crystal or glass bowl with pennies. Place the bowl in a well-traveled area of your home. Allow the bowl of pennies to remind you that you are working toward prosperity. Add pennies to the bowl often. When visitors come to your home share with them the concept of the penny bowl.

10. Visualize often the life of your dreams. Allow your intuition to lead you into new areas of interest. Try new things. Go to new places. Travel new roads. Develop new relationships. Intuitively seek new hobbies and aspirations.

11. Claim your prosperity today. Visualize your outer appearance as if you are living an affluent life. Now, create yourself as if you are the affluent individual you will soon become. Change your hair, makeup, attire, expression, and body language, if necessary.

12. Create a project that keeps your intuition focused upon prosperity. Begin to write a novel or short story about yourself.

Write of adventures and prosperous experiences that you encounter. This exercise will help you recognize the amazing power held within the ability to focus.

13. Love everyone. Love and respect and attempt to understand those of lesser and greater means. As you begin to love people who have discovered the secrets of an affluent life you will automatically lose any forms of jealously or intimidation that might be holding you back from reaching your goals.

Chapter Three Part Two-as channeled from the realms of magic, spirit, earth and angels

Working With Desire-as channeled from the magical realm

Think in terms of what you want instead of what you do not want. The amount of prosperity that is available to you will reflect your thoughts and desires. "I want to be loved and respected", is a positive thought instead of "I don't want to be ignored or taken for granted." Also, "I want an affluent life with the opportunity to drive a new safe car and wear attractive well made clothes," instead of "I don't want to be poor and have to drive an old junker and wear hand-me-down rags."

Desire is an amazing power. Your desire to create prosperity is a strong force that can be harnessed and used to attract that what you want. Desire is also your inner voice telling you what you want from life and what will make you happy. Desire is the key to prosperity when you listen to it because it will tell you what you want to be, what you want to do, what type of friendships are most compatible, and how you should look. Follow your desires and prosperity will come.

Individuals who are in touch with their own desire will usually get what they want because they have focused their goals and are willing to move toward these goals. Desire will cause you to adjust and reconstruct your present circumstances so that they are harmonious to your intuitive future projections.

Working With Human Connections-as channeled from the spirit realm

Your human connections are your most valuable assets. Indeed, they are the epitome of prosperity. Without simple human connections such as friendships, love, family, neighbors, community leaders and cultural exchanges you are alone and life ceases to have much meaning. Human connections are essential for happiness and prosperous attitudes. Intuitively you are driven to connect with like-souls. Connecting nourishes the soul and creates energy. Energy creates prosperity. You make human connections every day; when you smile at a stranger or say "hello" to a neighbor or when you open a door for an older person or say "thank you" to a store clerk you are investing energy in making simple human connections. We desire to laugh, converse, make love, and connect with souls of similar backgrounds and experiences.

It is essential to make deep intuitive connections with other human beings in order to be happy and to prosper. When you have connected passionately with another person your body and spirit speak to the Universe. You send signals to the world and those around you as to your personal desires. Instinctively, others will help you create the prosperity that you desire. The Universe picks up all positive energies and helps create that which you desire to be yours.

Working With Conversations-as channeled from the earthly realm

With human contact you can begin to speak about your inner desires. When you begin to converse with others you will begin to speak about your wants and needs. You will quicken the process of creating prosperity. Conversation is a way of releasing your goals and wants into the Universe as well as the minds of other affluent individuals. Affluent people are drawn to other affluent people. Connecting and conversing with others who have similar desires can be used as a system of sharing and act as a ritual that works to create that which we seek.

Conversation is a modern form of ritual; one where eye contact, body movement and voice energy are exchanged back and forth. Like a game of volleyball, conversation creates energy and creating energy is a ritualistic method of meeting your own needs. So, begin today conversing with others about your desires and you will soon see practical results.

Communicating Prosperity to Angels-as channeled from the Angelic Realm

Angels can clarify much that is concealed from us. We have learned, thus far, to utilize and trust five energy realms. The Angelic Realm is most helpful in creating prosperity. Angels work to keep order in the Universe. Angels are clarity and order and they make it possible for humans to connect to Godly order and clarity. You can ask the Angelic Realm today to help you organize yourself and thus create your future prosperity.

Like air, angels posses the power to flow within physical matter. Using angel energy, your thoughts and desires can overcome material restrictions and connect to higher vibrations giving you the power to gather your material needs. Angels have no preference toward your material wealth. You can be wealthy or you can be indigent and angels will continue to place you within the Godly order of things. But, because angels do not attempt to help you strive toward your own material wealth, you must be the one to take the first steps toward asking them for prosperity. Once you have asked for the vibrations of prosperity the angels will clarify and organize your efforts. Communicating with angels will begin your incline toward a prosperous life. Follow the exercises listed below to communicate with the angels.

1. Imagine or intuit the presence of angels; their color, smell, sound, emotions, appearance and name.

2. Attempt to feel the presence of angel energy. Are you feeling: protected, safe, loved, warmed, held, nurtured, watched and guided?

3. Use artistic abilities and methods to create angel impressions: intuitively splash colorful paint upon a canvas, freely move around the room, freely mold clay into an angel shape, photograph light and nature and write words upon paper.

4. Simply ask angels to guide you or your daily path, to enlighten you as to your destination, to help you with difficulties, to prepare you to grow and to accelerate the education of your soul.

5. Begin a savings account. Make a promise to yourself that you will put a designated amount into this special account each time you have a good day. You will find that your good days will grow and your savings will expand as well.

6. Develop a hobby that you really love. This hobby will grow and you will find that your talents grow too. As you become a more interesting person you will see more financial opportunities coming your way.

7. You are a confident individual with a higher destination. Begin to search for information concerning this higher destination. Talk to others who are spiritual and willing to offer advice. Your friendships are strong and they will support you and help you find your ultimate destination.

8. Using your psychic abilities plan a party and invite people who are willing to have fun and look for prosperity. Give the party a name that will attract prosperity. You could use, for example: Seekers of Affluence, Golden Dreams, Prosper for Prosperity or any other name that you like. Send out invitations explaining that you are a visionary with a desire to improve your life. Ask that only those who wish to improve themselves attend the party. You will be surprised to see who will and will not attend. Now, ask that every one bring one good prosperity idea to the party. The idea must be something that can be shared with others. Prepare a few snacks and drinks and let the party begin. You will be surprised at how

much fun you have and how quickly you find yourself in the company of positive and ambitious people.

9. Find a piece of silver or gold. A coin will work fine for this exercise. Polish the piece and repeat this affirmation: "Shiny stone of mineral good, Bring to me what you would. Shiny mineral of stony earth, Bring to me prosperity girth." Place the coin inside your front door. Only luck and good fortune will now enter.

10. As you attempt to fall asleep tonight, ask your angels to bring angelic vibrations into your body. Meditate and visualize angels and colorful auras. As you fall asleep you will begin to physically feel small vibrations pass through your body.

11. Tune into physical vibrations. As you ponder through your day, begin to notice that your body's energy level changes at different times in the day. Begin to tune into the changes you are feeling. Ask the angelic realm to work with you as you call angelic vibrations into your body. You will begin to experience sensations of hot and cool pulsing through your body.

12. Tune into the physical sensations of those around you. Watch family members and friends as they move through their day. Begin to empathize with their bodies. Watch with your intuitive eye and attempt to feel what others around you are feeling. You will begin to recognize that you are able to decipher the physical feeling of those around you.

13. Hone your skills. You are filled with expertise that you are not using. Don't let your abilities lie beneath the surface of your life. Pull them into the light and let them help you to be prosperous. You have the abilities to make the life that you desire right now. Go for it. Repeat this affirmation: "I can and will make the most of my ambitions and skills. I am a competent individual with no interest in the darkness of life. I will walk toward light and love. I will seek prosperity and I deserve it. God help me along the way."

You have begun to call into your life all that you want and need. Your intuition is stronger than ever and you are an amazing human being. You have many friendships, love and prosperity. You are in the process of developing a spirituality that fits your personal needs.

Chapter Four

Earth Spirituality

You are developing a beautiful and personal connection to the earth and nature; one that can help you create a spirituality and psychic abilities that will bring peace and happiness into your heart. The earth is plentiful with living and breathing attributes, just crying to be heard. She loves and nurtures all who live upon her. Like a mother, she gives a home, food and security to us. She exists within a complex system of planets and energies while providing a foundation for all creatures living upon her. Her energy, alive and vibrant, plays a role in psychic abilities and intuitions.

Nurturing a personal relationship with the earth and nature's energies will help you integrate selected aspects of earth energies into your spiritual belief system, as well as intensify your psychic connection to everything with which you come in contact.

In this chapter you will be introduced to the seasons and the opportunities they offer, as well as to a monthly cycle which influences the earth and everything living upon it. Using the information provided, you will be able to learn when it is best to make plans and changes in your life.

To begin a study of earth spirituality, it is necessary to first recognize the four seasons that affect the area in which you live. You enjoy four superb seasons; spring, summer, fall and winter. To learn about these miracles of seed planting, growth, life and death you need only to watch a planting season.

Each fall a miracle occurs outside of our homes. Trees and flowers drop seeds to the ground and two events begin. The flowering and fruiting season begins to wilt and die. In addition, the fruit and seeds of all fruits begin to create pregnancy within the earth as they drop. Mother Earth becomes filled with the seeds as she waits to give birth in the next birthing season. As winter approaches, the dead foliage fertilizes the earth and creates an enriched place for growing seeds. The winter, a time of sleep and nurturing awaits the coming spring. As spring appears, the new seeds begin to pop their heads out of the ground and the time of birth has arrived. Spring celebrates new fertility until summer approaches and a major growth session begins again.

A practitioner of earth spirituality recognizes the benefit of planting a row of corn and watching its' natural cycle of growth. The planting of any fruit, vegetable and grain acts as a phenomenal teacher. After a year and a day of watching a natural growth cycle, a practitioner of earth spirituality will have witnessed nature's entire growth aspect. Because you are connected to the same growing cycle you will discover that you are much like the fruit growing upon earth. In fact, you are a fruit of the earth.

Corn Crop

Of course, you should not make all decisions based upon the seasonal cycle but attempting to connect with the cycle will enhance your intuitive abilities as well as offer you a guideline as to when you might enhance key aspects of your life. It is said that Earth Spirituality should be studied a minimum of a year and a day in order that you might experience every season. The studying of the growth cycle of a corn crop will bring invaluable knowledge to the practitioner of Earth Spirituality. It is not necessary to plant more than a few grains of corn to begin your studies. Watch the crop as it changes and you will discover several patterns that only nature can reveal to you.

The Moon

Begin to notice the cycle of the moon. This cycle moves around a monthly pattern. You will notice that each month the moon begins and ends. In other words, it is born, lives and dies. The moon energies begin when the moon is in a dark phase. You will look into the dark sky and notice that the moon is not visible to your eye. This is the dark moon stage and a time when the moon is preparing to give birth in your home region and new fresh energy to you as well. As the new moon appears in the night sky, attempt to use your intuition to sense an increased power and energy that can be of help to you when beginning new projects. This energy is a real force that influences ocean tides and increased psychic energies. The moon will appear to continue growing in size and you will find that your energies increase even more. This increase in energy will continue until the moon appears full and bright.

Eventually a full moon will appear. The moon is filled with its greatest strength at this time, and you can utilize the moon's energies and draw the most energy from the moon at this time. You will be filled with optimal energy levels when the moon is full.

After the moon's appearance has grown to its fullest and brightest, it will begin to wane and you will begin to experience a decrease in energy. This is a good time to release stress and anxiety. The moon will grow smaller in appearance and its powers will continue to dwindle as well. Concentrate upon letting go of unwanted and unnecessary parts of your life at this time of the month.

Using the moon's monthly energy is a good way to stay connected with the natural energies available to you. Planning activities around these cycles will not only help you to become and remain connected to the Earth and her surrounding energies, but you will also begin to experience untapped vortexes of energy that will aide you in your everyday life and health.

Health

Natures' energies have the ability to rehabilitate old energies that lay dormant within your body. You have vortexes of energy pulsating within your body, at this very moment. Sometimes these energies can become stagnant and blocked due to stress, anxiety and poor living conditions. You have the key to unlock the wonders of these energies and connect with them today. Practice the following exercises along with keeping a good health regimen and you will see positive changes in both your mental and physical well being.

Natural Health Exercises

1. Practice deep natural breathing. Breath inward deeply but only to a comfortable point. Allow your lungs to fill with breath and release breath when you feel the need. As you continue this breathing exercise, visualize the healing colors of your aura moving into your lungs and than flowing back out again. Use your intuition to select your aura colors. Eventually you will find a color or mixture of colors that feels right for you. Continue practicing this breathing exercise and your intuitive abilities will become sharpened and sensitive to color. Also, using this breathing exercise will release stresses that may be causing energy blockages within your physical body.

2. After a full moon, when the moon energy is fading, find a quiet space to relax. Visualize the moon's appearance growing smaller while you visualize impurities present in your body growing smaller. If you close your eyes and look into the darkness with your mind's eye, you can see a mirror image of your body. See the image and look for impurities that might be present within the image. Once you have recognized these impurities (they could be disease, stress, bad memories, food deposits or negative emotions). Visualize them growing smaller and less threatening. Visualize the moon's appearance growing smaller too. When you

feel comfortable, imagine these impurities floating out of your mirror image and far away. See the impurities floating far into the universe, where they will eventually dissolve.

3. Visit an ocean at least one time each year. Spend time breathing the salty air and listening to the sound of the sea rolling upon the shore. Bathe your body in the natural salts of the sea.

4. Walk each day until you are comfortably tired. Your body and health are a reflection of spiritual health. Walking upon the surface of the earth helps bring physical strength and peace of mind. Make exercise a routine part of your life. As you continue to reflect upon the natural cycles of the earth and universe you will discover your own healing regimen as you become spiritually alive. As you live intuitively you will discover that you have instincts and a knowing which direct you toward a healthy lifestyle. Your spiritual life will unfold and communicate with Godly energies and nature. You will gnostically live and know the magic of the universe. Transformation of your physical body will follow this transformation of your spiritual self.

Because disease is prevalent in our society, it is easy to become sick with cancers and stress ailments. Once you have honed you clairvoyant sight, your spirit will be equipped to recognize your body's own healing signals. Your body will begin to communicate knowledge and your spirit will listen and understand. You will become one with the earth. To perceive oneself as whole and connected to nature is to be transformed in the spirit.

To further your growth and understanding of Earth Spirituality, you will find it helpful to acquire information about the growing cycles and properties of earth vegetation. Herbs are easily available and are a unique way of learning about earth vegetation. Each herb has a special property to share with you. The following list of herbs is categorized into sections: health, intuition and knowledge. Many herbs are grown and used for their specific healing qualities, while some are grown and burned to increase intuitive abilities, others are grown and consumed to aid in the acquisition of knowledge.

Intuitively, you will find herbs that you like and desire. You will be attracted to the herbal smells, appearances and the names of these herbs. Select one herb from the following list; purchase the herb. Watch it grow, and you will begin to learn about its growth cycle. It is not necessary to attempt to purchase or grow all of the herbs listed, however, after a while your intuition might help you become interested in herbs that are not listed. Add these new interests to the following list. Intuitively, you will know where to categorize your new find.

5.

Health	*Intuition*	*Knowledge*
Yarrow	Chamomile	Apple
Garlic	Cinnamon	Juniper
Celery	Basil	Vervain
Oats	Lemon Balm	Nutmeg
Orange	St. Johns Wort	Ginsing
Cabbage	Myrrh	Rosemary
Cayenne	Lavender	Raspberry

6. Rub your hands together until you feel a warm and tingling energy radiate from within. This warm energy is connected to the energy of the earth. It is real and tangible. Experience it often when you need a reminder that the earth is alive and has the ability to aid you in your psychic ventures.

7. Celebrate the changing seasons.

8. Ask the dream world to allow a familiar to come into your life. You will learn that a familiar is an animal spirit sent to you to offer

protection or to help with difficulties. When the dream world sends your animal familiar to you, take time to study and learn more about your familiar. If your familiar is a dog, think about adopting a dog. If your familiar is a cat, think about adopting a cat. If your familiar is an elephant, don't worry, you can visit him or her someday. Plan to meet your familiar and it will happen.

9. Study the directional energies created from the earth.

East: The east brings energies of new beginnings, inspiration and fertility. Eastern energies are strongest in the spring and in the morning hours. You can feel these energies most when wearing bright spring colors. These energies are transmitted through air and the sky. They are often called upon when a new venture is to begin or when inspiration and ideas are needed. They feel light and airy. They are breezy and quick. These energies are sometime responsible for fairies and flying creatures coming into your life. They fill the mouth with words and rule verbal communications. They are the energies most found in individuals who love to talk, sing, think and share information with others. A symbol of Eastern energy is the sword.

South: The south is hot and fiery. Southern energies are passionate and intense. They come into our lives when we have deep desires and need help to achieve them. It is easiest to connect with these energies in the summer months and in the mid day. The colors of the south are deep reds, gold and orange. If you seek to strengthen your will, you should call upon south energies. They are often seen in the form of lizards, dragons and desert animals. But don't be alarmed, these fire energies are not harmful; they have the ability to purify and clean. For example, after a forest fire, the ground is prepared to produce healthy new growth. This energy offers assistance to the east with its cleansing abilities. When air comes in, new growth follows. The east and south blend easily and make good fertility and rich soil. If you dare to play with fire, call the south into your life today. A symbol of the south is a burning torch.

West: The west is cool and wet, deep and filled with mystery. Like a dark ocean the west does not easily reveal its powers. Intuition is a fruit of the western energies. The west is most easily called upon in the fall and early evening. The colors of the west are bright aqua, greens and ocean blues, misty grays and lavender. If you are feeling unsteady you might be filled with too much west energy. West energy hits you like a wave and pulls you under if you are not careful; but under the surface, the secrets to all psychic questions are hidden. If you are in need of emotional tempering, call upon the west. She will come to you like a gush of cool water flowing over your body and you will be bathed in her magical touch. A symbol of the west is the chalice.

North: Silence! The northern energies come in the deep quiet of winter and near midnight. You can call upon them, but they will come only when they know you are ready. Wisdom is found here, but it is not given easily. Be silent and listen and you will learn to hear the north. Like a wise old crone, the north will come upon you when you least expect her, but she will be worth the wait. The main symbol of the north is a golden coin.

10. Plan a camping and hiking trip. Explore caves and forests. You will soon learn that the earth is more than you ever imagined.

11. Sleep when you are tired. Learn to respect the signals your body sends to you. Listen with an intuitive ear and sleep as much as you desire. Your body energy will heal itself as you sleep.

12. Plan a moon ritual. When the moon is full, go to a good restaurant with friends. Eat a big meal and remember as you eat that you are eating fruits of the earth. Experiment with lots of foods. Make a plan to have everyone order something different and share your meals. Do this with a feeling of adventure and good humor. You will have a great time and you will have tightened your relationship with the earth.

13. Write a prayer to the earth, giving thanks to her for all of the wonders that she offers. Learn to relate to the earth with reverence. Keep her clean and love her always. She will help you grow to be a spiritual being with much to share.

Your spirituality has been blessed and enriched. You are filled with inner strength and a spirit that cannot be easily disturbed. Like mother earth, you are wise yet soft and kind. You are a wonderful person and your life is better than ever. With all of the work that you have done, you are now ready to take a great step toward improving you psychic abilities and your new found spirituality will be with you along the way. As you continue along this path your psychic abilities will continue to grow. Indeed, it is time to give yourself a psychic reading.

Chapter Five

Psychic Reading

You are ready to learn to "read" for yourself and others. Your intuition is vibrating and striving to grow to its fullest potential. Just allow the psychic juices to flow.

A psychic reading is one where information is divined from intuitive forces. A psychic will have abilities that allow the past, present and future to been seen and told. Some psychic readers have adept abilities; they may see spirits, auras, images or visions. Other psychic readers may hear voices, sounds, words and information, while some experience a flow of information, or an intuitive knowing.

While many psychic readers use a combination of intuitive abilities it is the psychic who fully trusts and practices these natural abilities who will develop into a most proficient reader. You can do this with ease.

A psychic reading will bring information into the earthly realm where it can be useful to an individual. It is possible to give a psychic reading to oneself, and it is possible to give a psychic reading to others. There are four steps to follow when executing a psychic reading; clear, open, release and record.

Performing A Psychic Reading for Yourself

You will learn to execute a psychic reading to help divine helpful information from Godly energies. First, you must "clear" your mind from all thoughts and mundane information. It is easiest to clear your thoughts and mind by first relaxing your body. Take deep relaxing breaths with the intent to release the day's stress. Once you have relaxed your body your mind will more easily follow your directions. Next, ask your mind to relax and become clear and free of thoughts. You will become more capable of clearing your thoughts and mind with practice.

When you are ready, allow yourself to "open" your mind to the five Godly realms. You can connect with information from any or all of the Godly realms with practice and patience. To become open to these realms you must not judge what you see, hear or feel during a psychic reading. Pay attention to any and all signals that arrive. Recognize them and believe they are important. You might see a color, hear a noise, feel an emotion, see a vision, experience a memory, feel a pain, smell a scent, see an expression or shadow; the Godly realms might attempt to get your attention in any number of ways.

Stay "open" and begin to focus upon information that you desire to divine. Begin to focus upon a specific question. Ask the question out loud if your own voice helps you concentrate, or ask the question in your mind. You can ask questions that will lead you to a life of happiness and prosperity, a life of spiritual peace and contentment, or you can ask simple questions that will help you make simple daily decisions. Soon you will discover that your intuition will lead you toward the proper path, regardless of the questions you ask. The following questions will guide you toward an insightful reading.

Psychic Reading Questions

1. What aspects of my life are in need of revision?
2. How might I best institute changes in my life?
3. What aspects of my life are positive?
4. How can I better nurture my existence?
5. What purposes am I to pursue in my life?
6. Who are my mentors?
7. What are my strongest talents?
8. How might I obtain love?

9. What work am I to pursue?
10. Where is love available to me today?
11. Who am I to love today?
12. Why do I struggle?
13. Can I overcome struggle?
14. What lessons am I to learn?
15. What lessons am I to teach?
16. Am I on the path that is best for me today?
17. What changes must I make immediately?
18. Am I healthy?
19. How might I obtain optimum health?
20. How might I obtain optimum love today?
21. Are new relationships available to me today?
22. Is prosperity available to me today?
23. How might I improve the flow of love in my life today?
24. How might I improve aspects of relationships available to me today?
25. How might I create prosperity today?
26. What should I be doing today?
27. What spiritual messages are available for me today?
28. How might I improve my intuitive abilities today?
29. What is my connection to the earth today?
30. What is my connection to Godly energies today?

As information surfaces during the reading it is important to learn to "release" this information immediately. You will learn two methods to "release" information. It is best to speak-out-loud and repeat the information that has surfaced. Repeat what you have heard or say what you have seen. If you have seen a color or a vision, simply state the name of the color or the images in the vision. It is not your responsibility at this time to understand what the information is transmitting to you, but simply to repeat it. If you experience a memory during a reading, speak out loud the memory. You will notice at times during this process that when you open your mouth to speak, additional information literally comes out of your mouth. This process is called automatic speech.

Automatic speech is a process that many developed psychics use when giving a reading. It is a simplified process of channeling information flowing from the spirit world.

Another method used to "release" information is to write it down. It is suggested that you use both methods, speaking and writing, when you first begin to read for yourself. When writing the information you will learn to write only select words or phrases. You will eventually determine which words and phrases are most important to the outcome of the reading and than record them. However, as you continue this practice you will notice that often you begin to record additional information from an unknown source. You will notice that you begin to automatically write a word or phrase that you had not intended to write. Trust this process of automatic writing and continue writing until you have finished. This method of "release" is called Automatic Writing and it is simply a way for your body to connect with the spirit world.

As you divine information from your psychic reading "record" all sensations and information including simple ideas and thoughts as well as visions and voices you might encounter. Use the space provided in the Psychic Journal to "record" all psychic information you obtain during your reading. Your skills will grow as you continue reading for yourself and practicing the four basic principles of a psychic reading; clear, open, release, and record.

As you continue practicing and developing your abilities to give a psychic reading, you will find that this skill is helpful to you as you renew your life's circumstances. You can practice daily and you will become quite adept.

When you feel comfortable performing a psychic reading for yourself you may attempt a psychic reading for another individual. When you begin reading for others your psychic abilities will continue to grow quickly and intensely. It is important to be honest and positive when you give a reading to other individuals.

You should begin each reading by first speaking with your questioner. Help your query to feel comfortable. Inquire if your questioner has had a reading in the past. You might find that the questioner is afraid because of a past experience or you might discover that the questioner is bewildered as to what is expected during the reading. Often an individual seeking a reading does not know how to behave during a reading and would benefit from a few directions. The questioner might not know whether to ask questions or to remain silent. Conversing with the questioner will help ease any tensions. Let the query know that it is acceptable and often helpful if questions are asked.

When you feel comfortable enough with your skills to attempt to read for another person, begin the reading and "clear" your mind as you would do if you were performing the reading for yourself. Look for first impressions as you "open" yourself to begin the reading. If you have a first impression, you do not want to speak-out-loud at first. "Release" the first impression by stating it in your mind and record it there. When you are reading for another individual you must develop selected memory space where you release and record information that comes available to you during the reading. At first, this will be a challenge for you to learn, but with time it will get easier. If you have a hard time storing the information that becomes available, you could use paper and pencil to write the impressions. This will help you to remember what you are intuiting.

You will begin the reading by focusing upon a question the questioner asks or you will focus upon a question that you have chosen. If a questioner does not ask a question to start a reading you should begin the reading using one of two methods. Begin by asking a simple question. You could ask, "Why has this person come to see me today," or "What is troubling this individual", or "What new opportunities will come into this individual's life soon?" Do not verbalize these questions to the query, but as information comes forth I release it if it is positive. However, if the information is negative in nature, record it in a select section of your memory and attempt to release the information in a positive yet true manner. As all information has a positive aspect, it is possible to release information in a positive manner. An example of releasing psychic information positively follows:

Releasing Psychic Information Positively

Sandra's psychic reading reveals that she will be losing her job very soon. She has worked very hard to achieve the position and status that is hers'. She is admired by many of her coworkers due to the fact that her salary is one of the highest in the company. Without her job, Sandra would feel shattered and unworthy.

As Sandra's psychic reading reveals that her position will be taken from her it continues to reveal that Sandra will be very upset although she will spend only a short amount of time seeking a new position. Once she overcomes the initial shock and embarrassment of losing a good job she will begin to recognize personal abilities that she was unable to use in her "good job". She will begin to realize that other employers are very interested in hiring her and giving her even more responsibilities. Sandra will go to several interviews before making a decision. Eventually, she will chose a job that pays a little less than her previous position, but offers a greater since of accomplishment. Once Sandra is comfortable in her new position she will begin to make new acquaintances and eventually discover new interests and hobbies. When enjoying hobbies with her new friends she will discover that one of her new friends is her soul mate. She will be happy and grateful for the change in career.

Sandra is a lucky woman. She attempts to use her intuition to create the life of her dreams however; losing her present job will be difficult for her. A good psychic reader would not quickly blurt out to Sandra that she would be losing her present job. A good reader would not say, "Sandra, your job will be taken from you very soon. You will be very upset. It will be difficult for you to recover. You will have to go on many interviews before you get a new job. When you finally find a new job you will not be making the same money that you make today. Eventually, things will get better for you, Sandra but this will be a hard time for you".

A good reader would begin as follows, "Sandra, I see that you have changes in career coming you way. I can also see that you love your job very much and that you would not like to leave it, however, you will be moving toward better circumstances. It is true that your job will be coming to an end, but Sandra, the next job you take will be the job you are meant to have. You will feel upset about losing your job at first, but than you will realize that many things about this particular job were not right for you. Sandra, think for a moment about you job. Is it true that you are not using many of your skills? Is it true that you are not being given the opportunity to do many thing that you wish you could do in this position? After you have left you present position you will realize this. You will come to peace with this fact. In fact, you will be happy to look at many new opportunities. You will go to many job interviews and you will feel grateful to have the opportunity to choose a career that you love. You will eventually make a choice. It will be the correct choice. You will decide upon a job that pays less money than what you are making today but you will feel that prosperity for you is a life well lived. You will begin this new position and love it. You will make new friends because this new job changes you and your attitudes. You will discover new hobbies and adventures that you cannot see while you are employed in your present job. Once you have become comfortable in your new position you will find that it is the time to find love. Sandra, I can see that you will find your soul mate soon. But, Sandra, you cannot do this today. You will soon realize that leaving your present situation is a good thing. You have a wonderful life and good things coming to you.

After the reading, Sandra knows the information that was perceived psychically but she does not feel afraid. The psychic reading has taught Sandra to trust her intuition and the events that follow. Sandra is continuing to live the life of her intuitive dreams.

You must store the information that is coming available to you in your memory in order to see the whole story. After you have seen much of a situation you can begin to release it to the questioner. As you release the information to the questioner you will intuitively know what to say and how to release it. You will be able to talk with the questioner and give the questioner your first impression at this time, as well as any other psychic information you had stored in your memory. Talk freely now with your questioner and release all that you have perceived.

With practice, you will become a good reader. If your intentions are good the universe will work with you. You will learn with each reading that you perform. If you are truly called to give psychic readings to the public you will soon know it. The universe will let you know when it is time to begin reading for the public. You intuitively will know when it is time to read for the public.

Chapter Six

Prayers, Pleasures and Lavender

Lavender is a loving and healing spirit guide with the ability to share a multitude of magical energies. He is kind and patient and quite wise. I believe he is a healing spirit today, and must have been a powerful man who walked this earth at one time. We first made contact with each other several years ago. My stepfather had been traveling to Arizona right before his death in 1995. He had begun to send Native American relics back home. We were all delighted to get them. To me, he sent a beautiful card with an attractive young Native American woman hand painted on the front. Next, he sent me a few pieces of hand crafted jewelry; a ring and necklace, both handmade in a local Native American village. He explained that he had begun to enjoy visiting the local Native American villages; he had met many of their people and felt at peace there.

Back home, one week before my father's death, I went to bed and dreamed of Lavender, for the first time. Lavender, a strong and large built Native American man seemed to hover near my bedside. I slept but felt his strong positive presence. My right hand stretched out open as Lavender placed his hand upon mine. I could feel his smooth skin; radiating health and love. Even in my sleep, I could feel the presence of his energy. His hand, so strong yet so gentle, rested upon mine as if he were sending me strength. Lavender spoke only a few words, "Everything will be all right". Then he left. The next day I woke and talked openly of the dream. It was healing and powerful.

By this time, my intuition was quite strong. I was unable to see the signs of what was to come. Seven days later, while my father was visiting Arizona, he died, leaving our family devastated.

Lavender has been with me ever since. Sometimes many months pass without his presence but he always returns when there is a need. I have come to believe that Lavender's spirit was passed on to me from the Native American's of Arizona. I will always believe that he is a gift sent to me, from the spirit of my father. I often look back at the hand-painted card or the white gold jewelry when I need to remember my father, but Lavender comes and goes through my life quite often and I am secure that he will be with me always.

The following prayers and pleasures are his words. Have fun with them. They are simple messages of divine love and hopes of joy and happiness. Allow yourself to be lighthearted and happy as you read through his reflections. Be free from judgment and seek only pleasure as you attempt to integrate his practices into your lifestyle. He will share herbal recipes, loving words to God, seasonal rituals, magical charms and even a few glimpses of life through his eyes.

His methods can help bring your dreams to fruition if you attempt to see life through his eyes. You will find joy and pleasures along with laughter and light, through the following magical prayers, pleasure-invoking stories and unusual but authentic photographs of spirit forms that Lavender has chosen to share with you. As you glance at the photographs provided, remember that magic is the ability to believe in miracles. Believe in magic and you will be transformed.

Bring Lavender into your home, and your life will change for the better. If you desire to share in his energies and welcome him into your life, his energies will appear. His beauty and vision will be yours.

Lavender's Spirit Forms-photographed by sHEALy

Lavender's Unicorn Tree

Beside a well-traveled road, in Maryland, a horse farm exists, still to this day. Young colts and their mothers often run and play with little care as to the busy world just a few hundred yards away.

One single tree stands in the center of this plush field. Often the loving horses rub their backs upon the tree and lean upon its side while humans zoom past performing their busy routines. The beauty of nature, the birth of young life and the shabby old tree just keep playing in their natural way as humans look away.

The tree stood strong for a few years and the horses grew wiser and more young foals appeared. But still, the cars filled with busy humans drive past, even faster now.

The town grew into a city and buildings rose from the edge of the field but the tree and horses did not mind. In fact, they seemed to be happy and content in their own little world when Lavender guided me to notice the miracle that was taking place right there on the side of the road.

Lavender, with his fun loving spirit, guided me to this field one rainy summer day. It was raining hard; the skies were gray and the traffic was calmer than usual when I pulled my car to the side of the road. Before I got out of the car, I noticed the shabby old tree and a smile came to my lips. The horses had left the field now, to escape the cold rain but the shabby old tree remained marking the spot where they would soon appear.

This shabby old tree, filled with the spirit of nature and the power of the horses it had lived with, for so long, has changed its form as the years have passed. Now, standing before my eyes in the center of the field a beautiful wooden horse grows from the top of a stump. Through the rains and winds and hot summer days, the spirit of the tree has emerged. The tree has faded but its true spirit is left, with a horn on its head, a body reared toward the heavens; with a head held high, a beautiful unicorn now stands.

The horses still play near the shabby old tree, but the shabby old tree does not stand out so much anymore. As I pass the tree, so often now, I seem to notice a happy mood and message speaking to me. "I'm one of them now. I'm anything I want to be," says the shabby old tree.

Visualize Lavender Earth Spirit, Here

One fall evening the spirit of Lavender visited me and a group of friends during a fall equinox ritual. I was celebrating in an open field with a group of friends; the daylight was fading and the moon was climbing high in the sky. A group of friends and I decorated the field with fall colored streamers, small twinkling lights and dried lavender. We started a fire and a slight breeze in the air stirred the fire that was growing in our fire pit. We were excited to celebrate the harvest time of the year.

A small silk blanket, placed in front of the fire, was decorated with lighted candles, corn cakes, crystals, amethyst and goblets when we sat down in a circle, ready to begin our celebration. We held hands and closed our eyes, listening to the gentle strumming from our guitarist and the steady beat from our drummer's drum. One of the men present spoke a meditation. His voice was calm and smooth. He asked us to visualize the field that we were sitting upon, growing wild with flowers and fruits. I began to visualize the field overflowing with wild berries and sunflowers and I started to relax, the day's tensions melting away.

Listening to the meditation helped me to open my psychic channels, and I began seeing colors and smelled strong aromas as I listened to his peaceful words. I breathed deeply and felt myself relax into a trance. All of us were peaceful now. The night was still and beautiful as the clear sky sparkled from above our heads. We visualized the field, and than the earth, growing strong and healthy. All of us, committed to improving the environment, attempted to call upon healing energies.

When the meditation led us to open our eyes we looked at the fire growing within the center of our field. It was bright and golden, warm heat radiated from the fire upon our faces. Everyone was quiet for a while until I felt the urge to speak. It was customary to share insights at this time so I spoke to the group and told them about Lavender, the spirit. Everyone listened as I shared with them my connection with the strong and healing Native American spirit. As I spoke, one of the others picked up a few pieces of dried lavender and threw it into the fire as a sign of gratitude.

The fire began to crackle and caught our attention. Again, someone picked up a few pieces of the dried lavender from the ground and tossed it happily into the golden fire, now raging even higher. We all watched and felt delighted as a golden form appeared from nowhere and danced within the fire. The pit seemed to glow brighter as a human form emerged.

Everyone knew at that very moment that Lavender was attempting to visually connect with us. He was sharing his healing energies so that we might grow stronger and share ours. The fire continued to burn and Lavender continued to dance for about seven minutes until the energy subsided. Once again, Lavender had emerged and presented a healing message to the world.

Visualize Lavender Fire Spirit , Here

Lavender's Incantations and Recipes

Lavender's Apple Charm Incantation

The fruit of the gods in her lush and green tree ripens to call and tempt the entire world to see. She begins as a seed. She grows full and complete. The fruit of the gods can bring only good deeds. If you desire the birth of moral values in the community in which you live, you can make happy gifts for your family to give. Plant an apple tree not too far away and watch as fruit arrives on a sunny spring day. Tell the neighborhood children what you have dreamed and they too will welcome your charming tree when it's big. Your desires will grow through the community source. The children will gather and watch the tree growing, of course.

When your tree finally matures and her fruits have grown ripe you bring the apples inside and you sort them by type. The big ones for happiness and the small ones for dads. The round ones for mothers and the flat ones for the lads. You bake some and dry others, you polish those to can. You send some in baskets you put some in jam. Your dreams of morality have certainly grown. You've started a practice that makes your name known.

Lavender's Mint Oil Recipe

Spearmint is an herb that is easily grown in a pot or backyard. Its light green color is attractive to the eye and its fuzzy flower-like buds are entertaining when used to decorate any dinner table. Mint in a backyard will grow and spread quickly. When planted in an area that can be mowed. mint makes a thick carpet of short fragrant plants. Mint is a home helper because it keeps rodents away. When new mint sprouts in the early spring, make cuttings of the new leaves. Bring the new leaves inside, wash them and let them air dry in a cool area. Once the fresh mint leaves are dry and clean, chose a healthy vegetable oil; bring the oil to a warm temperature and than add the mint leaves to the warm oil. Keep oil covered and let it cool naturally. When the oil is cool uncover the oil and let the mint leaves remain in the oil for 10 to 15 hours. Remove the mint leaves from the oil and close place oil in a clear bottle. Tightly seal the bottle and refrigerate. The cold oil will make a healthy cooking oil. Using mint oil will help quicken digestion and freshen breath.

Lavender's Sage Stick Recipe

Grow sage in a pot inside your home. Its properties are healing and magical. In midsummer, cut leaves from sage and place them on a cookie sheet. Preheat your oven to warm. Put the cookie sheet into the warm oven and let the leaves dry until they are stiff. Do not over dry the leaves; they should not crumble. Once the leaves are stiff, gather them and begin rolling them on a table beneath your hands. Roll back and forth until the leaves bind together. Using a thin green cord, wrap the sage leaves into a pencil shape. Place the wrapped sage stick in a sunny cool area allowing it to dry further. It will take your sage stick approximately one to two weeks to completely dry. Once the stick has dried completely you will be able to burn the end of your stick several times. The smoke from your stick will cleanse your home of negativity and illness.

Lavender's Thoughts

Lavender's Dream Forest Vision Quest

You feel leaves crunch under you feet. The sky overhead is speckled with stars. Your home is far away and the night embraces you. Crickets sing from the distant hillside to the sound of your footsteps. You stop, stand still and smell the dewy air. The forest is your retreat. The wool blanket, unfolded, makes a perfect bed. The warm breeze caresses your skin and sleep comes easily. Filled with an operetta of vibrations your dreams lift you through treetops and distant city lights. High above the sleeping homes and darkened streets you float among the other dreamers. Nature spirits come alive from inside old tree trunks, while fairy creatures unfold their wings and fly from fairy mounds. Multiplicities of power animals smile through brilliant sharp teeth. The night bursts into being. Your lessons begin....

Morning comes. Sunlight spots through tree tops. You wake to a canopy of greenery overhead. The air smells of fresh herbs and lime grass as you stroll toward home with a faint memory of the dream.

Spend a night in the forest!

Lavender's (unedited) view of Spirit Realm

Spirit world is large, very large. Many spirits wait to pass over. Many will not pass, but most will.

Spirit can choose. There is free will in spirit world. Spirits will choose to come back to earth or to pass over into the next realm.

Some, like me, are workers and guides and healers; they stay here, in spirit world, for eternity.

Spirit world is beautiful. It is alive. Spirit is alive more after death. Spirits are forever. There is no end.

I will not pass over into the next realm. I choose spirit world. I will stay. I will work. I help many. My work is good for you.

I am spirit for eternity. I live always.

Humans do not see me, always. They don't look. Only some, see me. They look with their heart. They teach with heart. They see me and then they teach and heal. They see me because they love.

Many humans have lost their spirit. They do not love anymore. They have dead spirit. They must learn to love. They will go to spirit world and learn. The spirit will come back to them. They will find what they have lost. They will learn love.

In spirit world they will see everything. Everything will be all right. They will see with their heart. Love will come to them.

Everyone finds love. Everyone finds spirit.

Spirit world is in trees and flowers, and corn and animals, rock, earth, sky....

Spirit is blue and gray and lavender in your human body. If you have strong spirit, you have strong color. Strong spirit flows into sky. It is all around you.

Human body loses spirit at death. Body turns to brown ash. It feeds earth. Spirit is free to fly. Spirit flies fast. Blue and gray and lavender comes to spirit world. It floats out of ash body, then comes to spirit world. If man is ready to die, you see his gray spirit in his face. He is gray. His hair and skin are gray.

He can choose to go back to Mother Earth. If he chooses to go back earth, he must wait. He changes and then travels back to physical earth. Spirit waits for birth.

Many spirits pass over to angels. Spirit stays with angels. Spirit becomes love; angel love. Spirit is love forever. Spirit will not go back to earth in physical body. Spirit comes back with angels.

Angel love is good. It is God. Angel love is always. Everywhere you see angel love. You have angel love in you, now.

You can be angel love or spirit or you can go back to earth. You have free will to choose. You will choose soon.

Lavender Answers Questions (unedited)

Lavender, what is clairvoyance?

Clairvoyance is a gift of sight. Many humans have the gift. Some can see into other realms; see future, auras and spirit guides.

What can I gain by enhancing my clairvoyant abilities?

Work to find your abilities. Open to natural experiences that are around you. Nature teaches you about your self. You are connected to Nature. All are a part of Nature. There is a natural cycle. Your sight will help you heal and teach. You must heal the earth. You must teach others to heal the earth.

What is Earth Spirituality and how will it benefit me?

Belief is good. Earth Spirituality is belief. the natural process of the Earth is good. It is healing. Belief and spirit is earth spirituality. It loves the sky, sea, fire and earth. Earth Religion is spiritual knowing of earth. It is up to you to heal Mother Earth.

I have animals. Can I use my intuition to better understand them?

Yes, it is the best way to understand animals. Animals have a natural intuition. They know you and you can know them. Connect with an animal using intuition. They will talk to you. You will grow.

Do I have a Spirit Guide?

Spirits are everywhere. You can find the spirit world, now. Yes, you have one Spirit Guide, maybe more. Spirit is with you. Listen to spirit. Stop making noise. Spirit is talking to you.

Lavender, what are angels?

Angels are the purest form of Godly energy. They are next to God. Their energy is fast; moving like lightning and rain. Angels will stay with God forever. They are God's will and intentions.

Lavender, I know a child who has died. Why must children die?

Children are spirits. Many have passed into spirit world. Some leave the earth to teach other human about love and life. Other children leave the earth because their bodies are ill or poor. Most leave because they need to be in spirit world again. Spirit would is beautiful. It is filled with love. All children have free world in spirit world. They can stay here in spirit world or the can go to the angel realm. Some children can go back to earth after many many years. Children live again on earth or with God's angels. They must not stay here in spirit world forever.

Lavender, why is it that some couple cannot have a baby?

The physical body is imperfect sometimes. It does not respond as it is created to do, sometimes. Many couples can not produce a physical body of an infant. This is harmful the their spirit. This causes great pain. These couples must realize that they too are parents. They are spirit parents. Their child will incarnate into another body. The child will eventually find them. They will eventually find the child. Today, many couple chose adoption. This is a good thing. Many spirits incarnate into the body of an infant and wait to be found by their true spirit parents.

Lavender, how can I find my life purpose?

All human have a purpose to learn, love, teach and heal. Your specific life's purpose will begin at one of these roads. Do not fear your life's lessons and you will learn to love. Embrace all things. All things lead to God. Do not fear love and you will learn to teach. Do not fear teaching others and you will learn to heal. Then, you will find you life's purpose.

Lavender's Prayers

Lavender's Baby Fertility Incantation

You want to have a baby soon. You hope to find her in this tune. There is a special way, you see, to bring the baby soon to be. First, plan to meet that special one with true love that feels like fun. Make magical love with that special one and baby will eventually come. But, magical love is not like the rest. Magical love is truly the best. It starts out small and turns to grand. Magical love only real lovers can understand. It's not what happens just for fun. It's not what happens with anyone. Magical love only comes sometimes. Magical love can't be found in rhymes. You must take that special one and begin to have a little fun. Go into the park today. Go into the woods to play. Let your worries disappear. Only happy moments should be clear. When you have found that special one, you must enjoy each other as one. When the baby feels the joys of today; it will be time to buy baby toys, hooray.

Lavender's Dear God Prayer

Dear God, I learned to pray in a very special way, to bow, my head and bend my knees; Dear God, so that you can hear me. But now I'm told it is okay to speak to you any part of my day. I might be busy or over stressed and yet this time could be the best. Dear God, I'll pray that special way, but God, I too like this new way. I can find you in a churchyard or I can find you in my back yard. Dear God, it's wonderful to see that you will always look after me. So, I think I need you right now and I must reach you somehow. I need to know you are always there. I need to find you everywhere.

Lavender's Seasonal Celebrations

Lavender's February 2 Incantation

Burn orange or yellow candles in celebration of the sun. The sun is growing stronger and the days are growing longer. Be aware of the energy of the Sun. As you gaze into the candles, visualize the sun's energies seeping into your body. The energy of the Sun is powerful. Our earth depends upon this energy. Honor and respect it. Sprinkle lavender around your home. The scent will keep you intuitive and strong.

Lavender's March 22 Incantation

Spring is returning. New growth is abundant. This is the time of inspiration and new beginnings. Plant seeds in your garden to celebrate the spring. Wear bright colors and sing today. Spring is in the air. The color lavender will spring up everywhere. Pay special attention to this color today. Let it remind you that life is good and magic is in the air.

Lavender's May 1 Incantation

Celebrate fertility and love. Make love. Dance. Sing. Laugh. Be happy. Have fun. Make the day a special one. This is a time when nature is the most fertile. Celebrate with wine and good food. Breathe in spring scents. Wear lavender colors. Fall in love.

Lavender's June 21 Incantation

This is the longest day of the year. Light is most powerful, but tomorrow darkness will begin to grow. Honor the light and accept the night. Pick June flowers. Appreciate their beauty. Celebrate the cycles of birth and death as you watch the June flowers begin to wither. Burn lavender candles in celebration of this day.

Lavender's August 1 Incantation

Celebrate the coming harvest. Summer will soon pass. Darkness and cold are on their way. Watch the Sun as it sets, see darkness cover your hometown. Be prepared to sleep peacefully and dream. Harvest lavender today. This is the time of the year when the lavender plant is ready to be harvested.

Lavender's September 21 Incantation

The harvest is here. Day and night are of equal energies. Celebrate balance and peace of mind. Be grateful for all that is balanced and calm in your life. Walk the Earth today with prayer upon your lips. Burn lavender incense.

Lavender's October 31 Incantation

The Spirits are close tonight. Celebrate the spirit world. Dress in costume and have fun. Remember those who have passed into the Spirit Realm. Meditate and look for spirit guides. Sleep with lavender under your pillow tonight. Spirits love lavender.

Lavender's December 23 Incantation

This is the longest night of the year. Tomorrow the sun's energies will begin to grow stronger. Respect the night's gifts, but look toward the return of the sun's gifts. Celebrate the darkness. Watch the skies for bright stars. Make a purchase today. Find and buy lavender seeds to be planted during the next growing season.

Allow these rituals to embellish your life. Rituals are a fun way to celebrate the earth and special occasions. Have fun with them. Trust them to help you grow to be a more prosperous and successful person. Plan parties around these holidays; invite friends over to celebrate the seasons. Watch your friendship base as it grows and grows and grows, just like lavender.

Your intuition is blooming and so are you!

Part Three

THE JOURNALS

The following pages are blank, waiting to be filled with your unique and private reflections. They are your journals, have fun with them. They will become special rituals helping you discover your inner voice and visions. Record your dreams, important thoughts and all psychic activities. As you begin to use these journals, your intuitive voice will speak to you. Write freely and believe in the power of your intuition. The power to believe is necessary and a commitment you must make today.

Begin now. Write in your journals, visualize yourself as a powerful and confident human being. See yourself as a person growing and learning to love and live a wonderful and new life. Believe that life is good. Expect greatness!

Reach deep into your inner self. Pull out the unexpected. Record it. Hold it close to your heart.

After you have filled your journals, put them away for a while. Live your life to the fullest. Continue to live using your intuitive voice. Then, go back to your journals and read them again. Your intuitive voice will come alive on the pages.

Chapter Seven

Your Psychic Journal

_____
_____
_____
_____
_____
_____
_____
_____
_____
_____
_____
_____
_____
_____
_____
_____
_____
_____
_____
_____
_____
_____
_____

Chapter Eight

Your Dream Journal

_____
_____
_____
_____
_____
_____
_____
_____
_____
_____
_____
_____
_____
_____
_____
_____
_____
_____
_____
_____
_____
_____
_____
_____
_____
_____
_____
_____
_____

Chapter Nine

Your Thought Journal

CONCLUSION

Congratulations to you, who have made the decision to create a better life for yourself. You, undoubtedly have already become a living example of success in the eyes of those around you. You are an insightful person with much to give others. Your goals are now clear in your mind. You have made the decision to live a happy and successful life; one that involves prosperity, loving relationships, a satisfying career, good health and a comfortable spirituality. These things are the quintessential ingredients to the life that you are choosing to live. Always, make these goals a top priority.

Continue to dream your dreams, laugh and have fun while looking at life through your own intuitive eyes. You will not be disappointed with your present or future life if you stay connected to the five Godly realms, use your imagination, your intuition and continue to believe that a happy life is yours for the taking. Your intuition is your good sense and good judgment. Trust yourself to create a beautiful destination. You are growing at this very moment.

Keep focused on your goals. Because many people do not remain focused on their goals, they often do not keep the intuitive powers that they first obtain when beginning their intuitive journey. It is important to often come back to the exercises in this manuscript; refocus and begin the journey again and again. Each time the results will be amazingly more powerful and your depth of intuition will increase. Many individuals at first, open their intuitive channels and experience exciting revelations and positive changes in their attitudes and lives, but eventually, after some time, they allow their intuitive channels to close. We are creatures of habit and it is important to often return to these original teachings and exercises in the attempt to change old habits into new and productive ones. We must create new habits and continue to integrate these intuitive exercises and attitudes into our daily lives. We must force old habits to disappear as new habits forms. So, keep working toward enlightenment and the pursuit of happiness.

While working through this manuscript, you have created and eaten great meals and listened to the best of music and you have met with spirits from the other world. You've seen magic and the results it can bring you, and you have become determined to have the life of your dreams. Intuition is now your leader along a path of splendor. You have begun to use intuition as a natural means to get what you want and deserve. While you met the five Godly realms you experienced the collective unconscious, angels, spirits, nature and psychic phenomena. You learned that enlightenment is simply the pursuit of happiness, and today you are determined to be a happy human being. Yes, you are one of the enlightened ones now.

You have learned that you must share with others the wisdom that has been gifted to you. When we give of our wisdom we create positive changes in the Universe and we become open to newer information and a continuation of positive happenings in our lives as well.

This manuscript is my attempt to share goodness with the world, with those who are willing to stretch their belief system enough to know what only the intuitive eye can see. While writing this book, my intuition flowed freely. My intuition helped me chose the material that eventually found its way into this book. Everything you have read here, is basic information, produced for the general public. It is a first step toward bettering your life. Keep using your intuition and magically, it will grow.

Share the information that you have learned with others, when it is possible. Encourage others to read 'Living Your Intuitive Dreams', and begin their own pursuit of happiness. As you help others recognize their intuitive possibilities you will be expanding your own life and continuing to create the life of your own intuitive dreams. Perhaps, you will find your path leading you in the direction of teaching others to live their dream life.

Whatever path you chose, you are on the right path because you are living with new goals and the tools in which to create these goals. You are extraordinary and loving and you deserve the best life has to offer.

Thank you for becoming a part of my intuitive journey. If you would like to share with me your intuitive experiences, please e-mail me at maryandtinsel@home.com. I cannot promise that I will answer every e-mail, but I will read each one. While teaching my workshop 'Living Your Intuitive Dreams', I often share short stories that have been sent to me after changing the names of the participants. So, look for your story in my next book.

If you are interested in becoming a certified 'Living Your Intuitive Dreams' group leader, or if you are interested in scheduling a 'Living Your Intuitive Dreams Workshop" in your home town, a list of classes and opportunities will be made available to you.

Bless you, and live with love!

©sHEALy 'Living Your Intuitive Dreams'
10-10-01

The following pages are intuitive answers to your everyday questions. When you have a question, flip through the pages and find the answer! (just for fun)

Not today, but soon.

Discover your inner voice.

Yes, there are good things in life.

Everything has a meaning.

A life lived without competition is not always the best.

Friends are always a good investment.

Love is the best answer.

Yes!

No!

Today is the best day to begin.

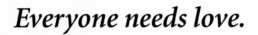

Everyone needs love.

Discover a new road.

Listen with you inner ears.

It's time to ask the angelic world.

The season will be your guide.

A soul mate is sometimes hard to find.
Keep looking.

Love is in the air.

Look up. The answer is there.

Yes, you can do it!

A new season begins soon.

Watch out!

Keeping looking up!

Don't stop.

Tears are a part of life too!

Friends are everywhere. Find some new ones.

Eat your vegetables.

Spirits walk with you.

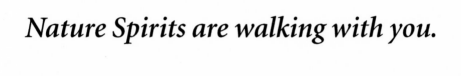

Nature Spirits are walking with you.

Printed in the United States
1242600003B/141

9 780595 208074